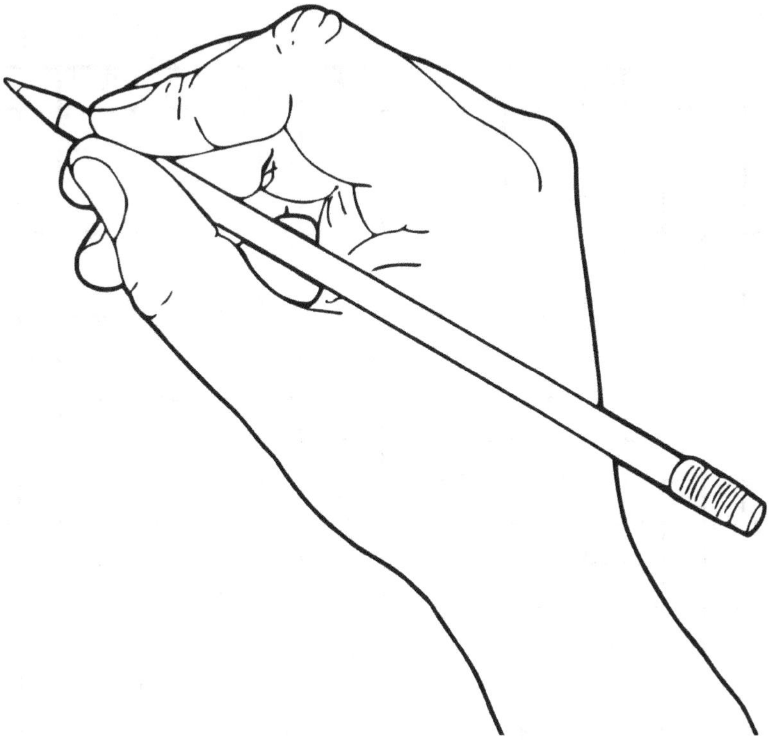

This Notebook belongs to:

____

MAZE

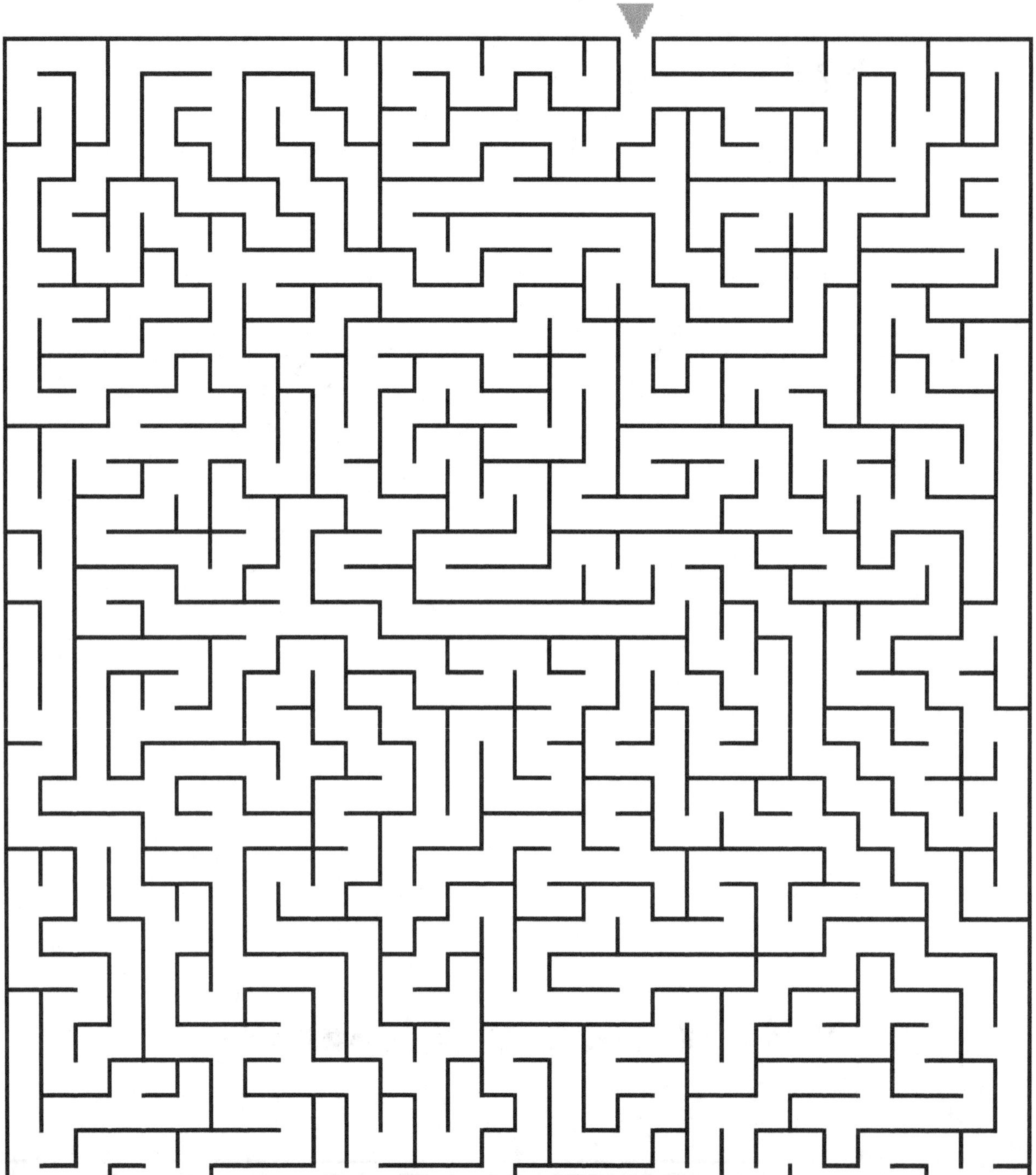

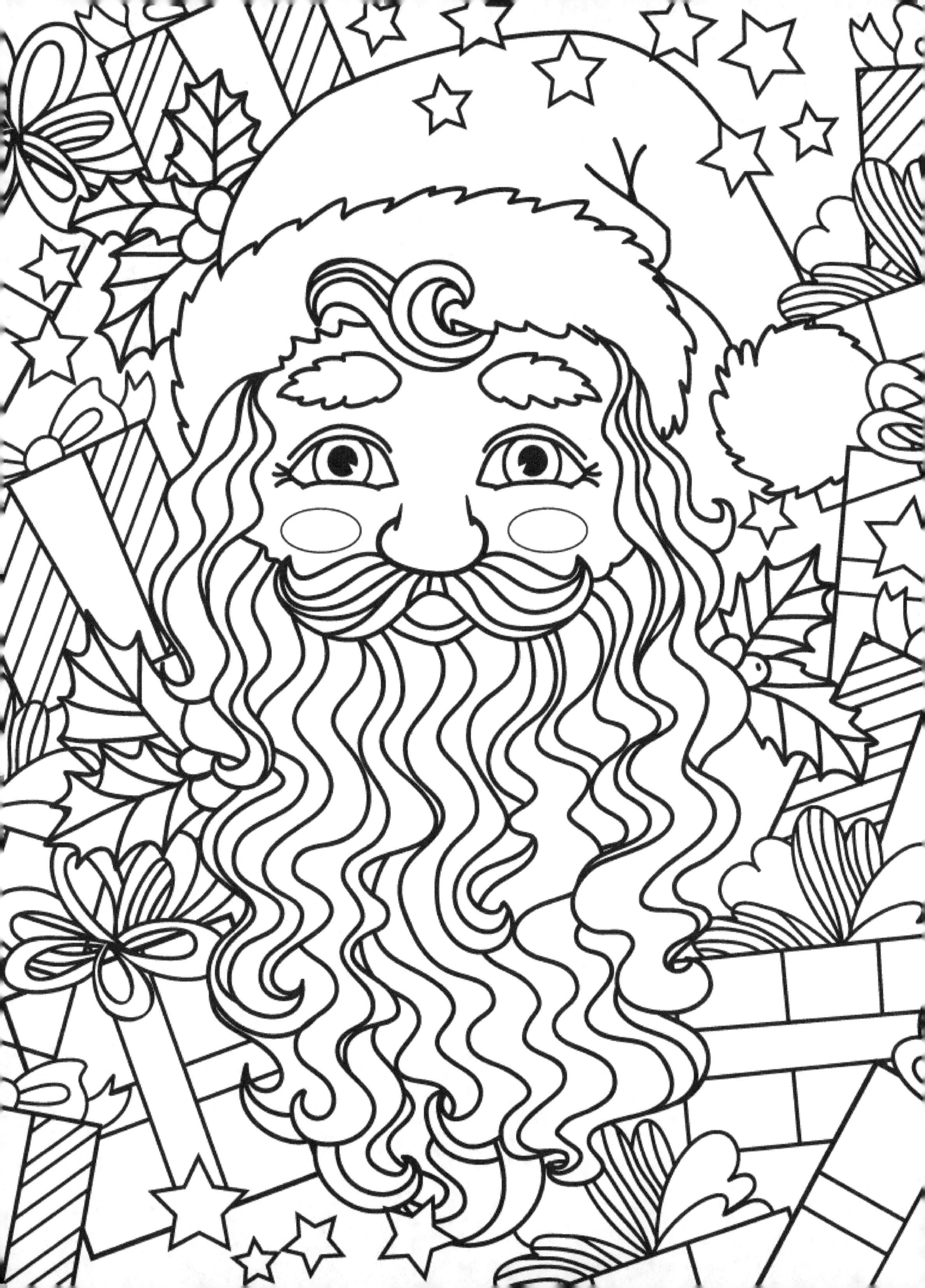

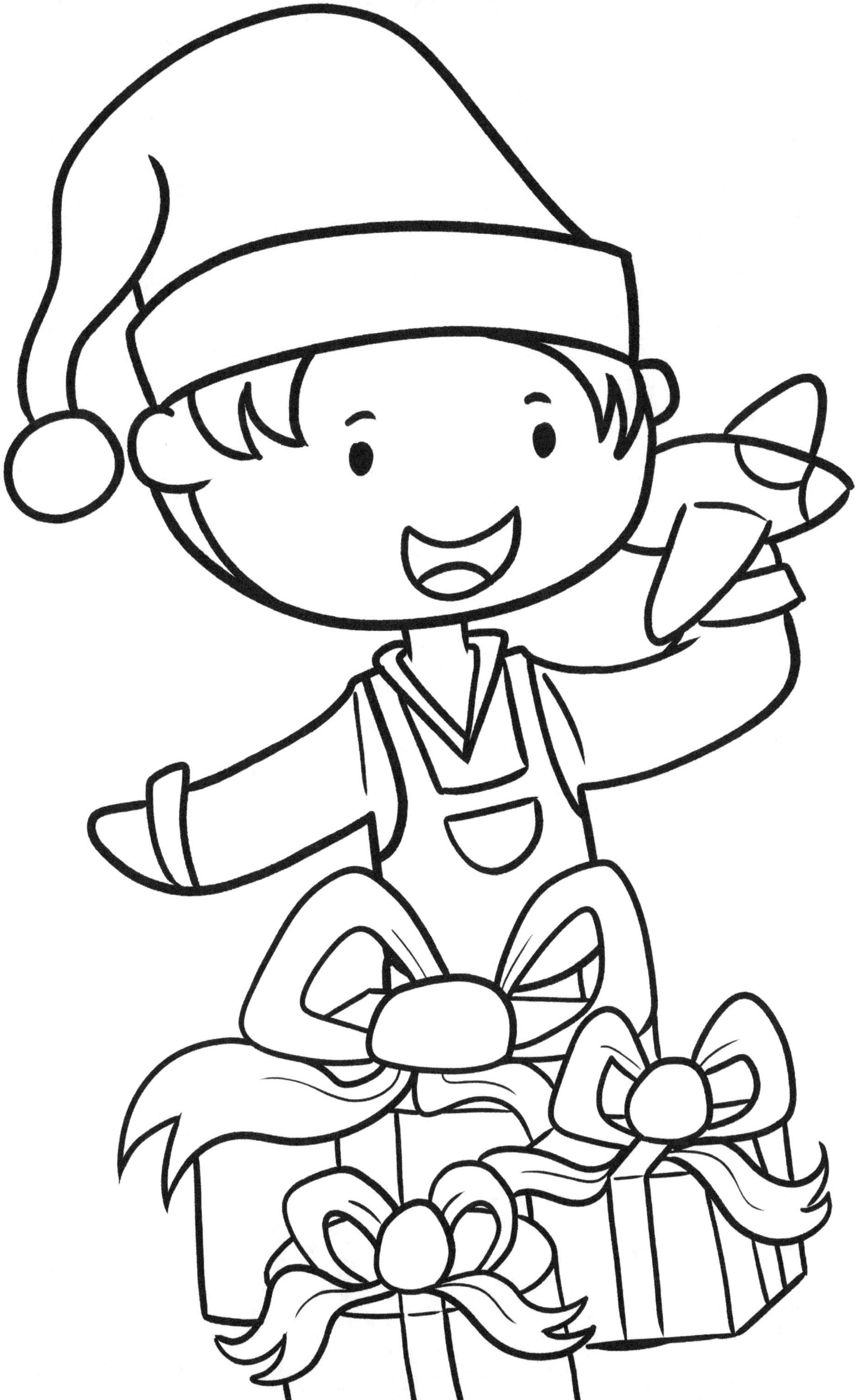

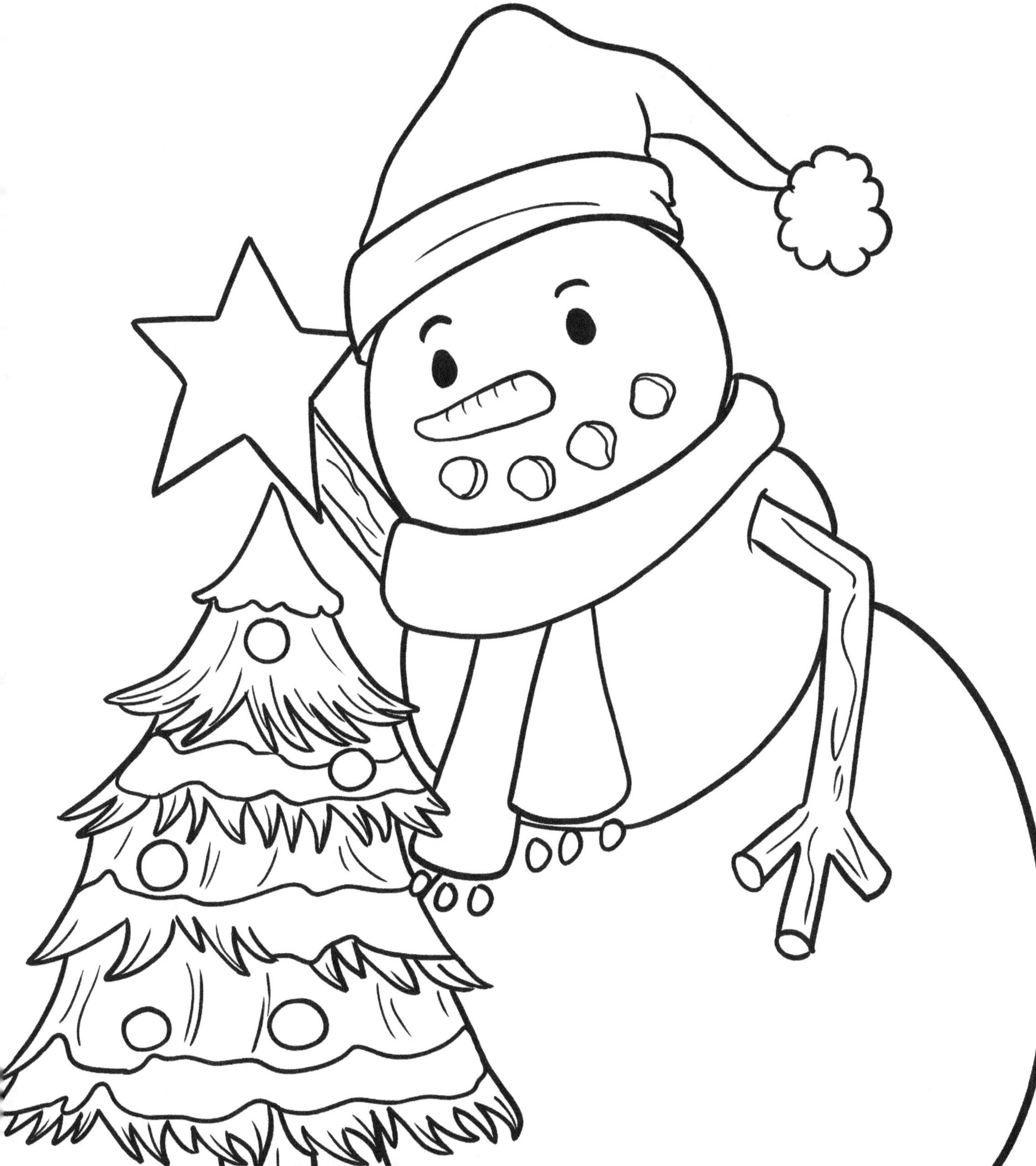

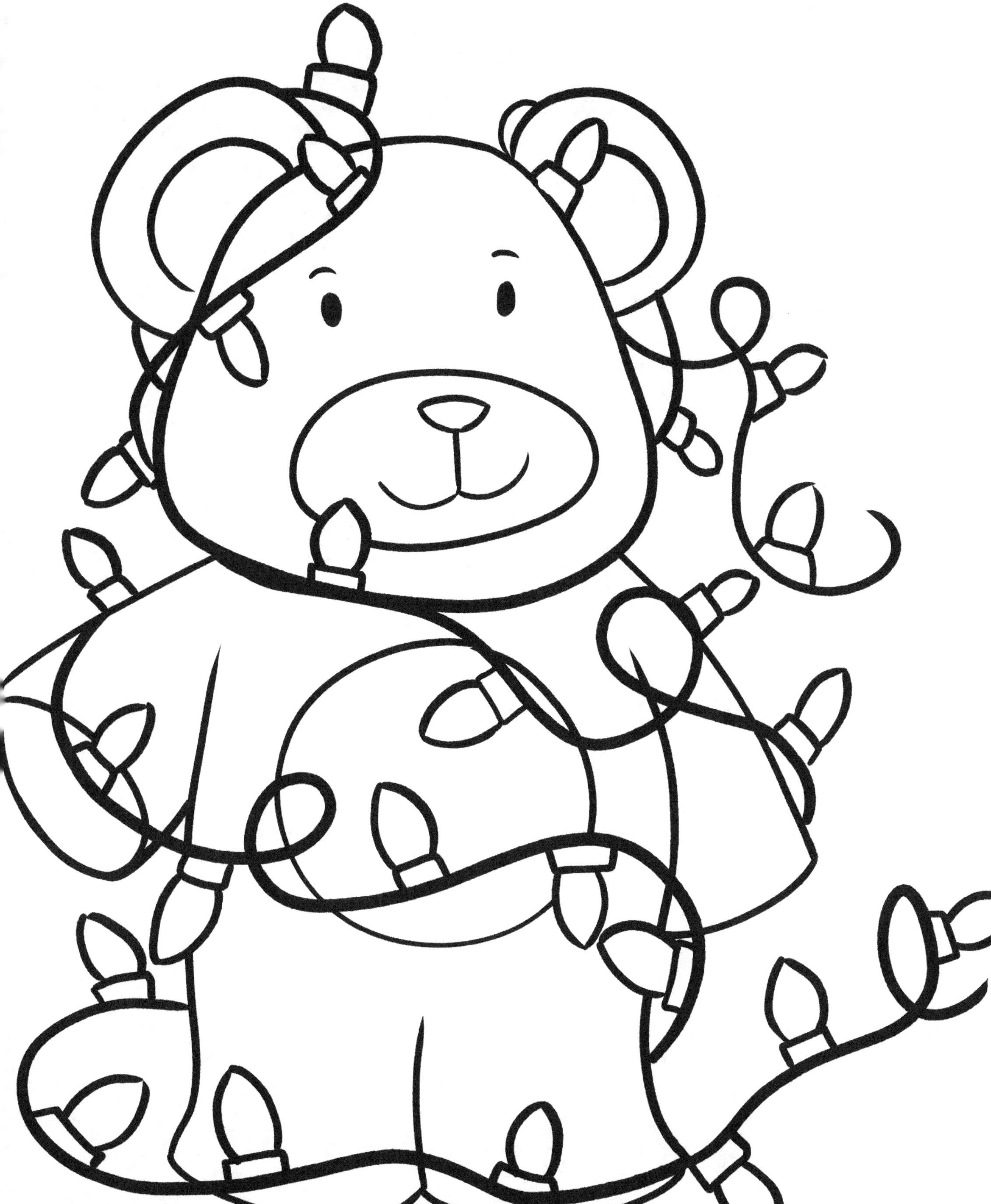

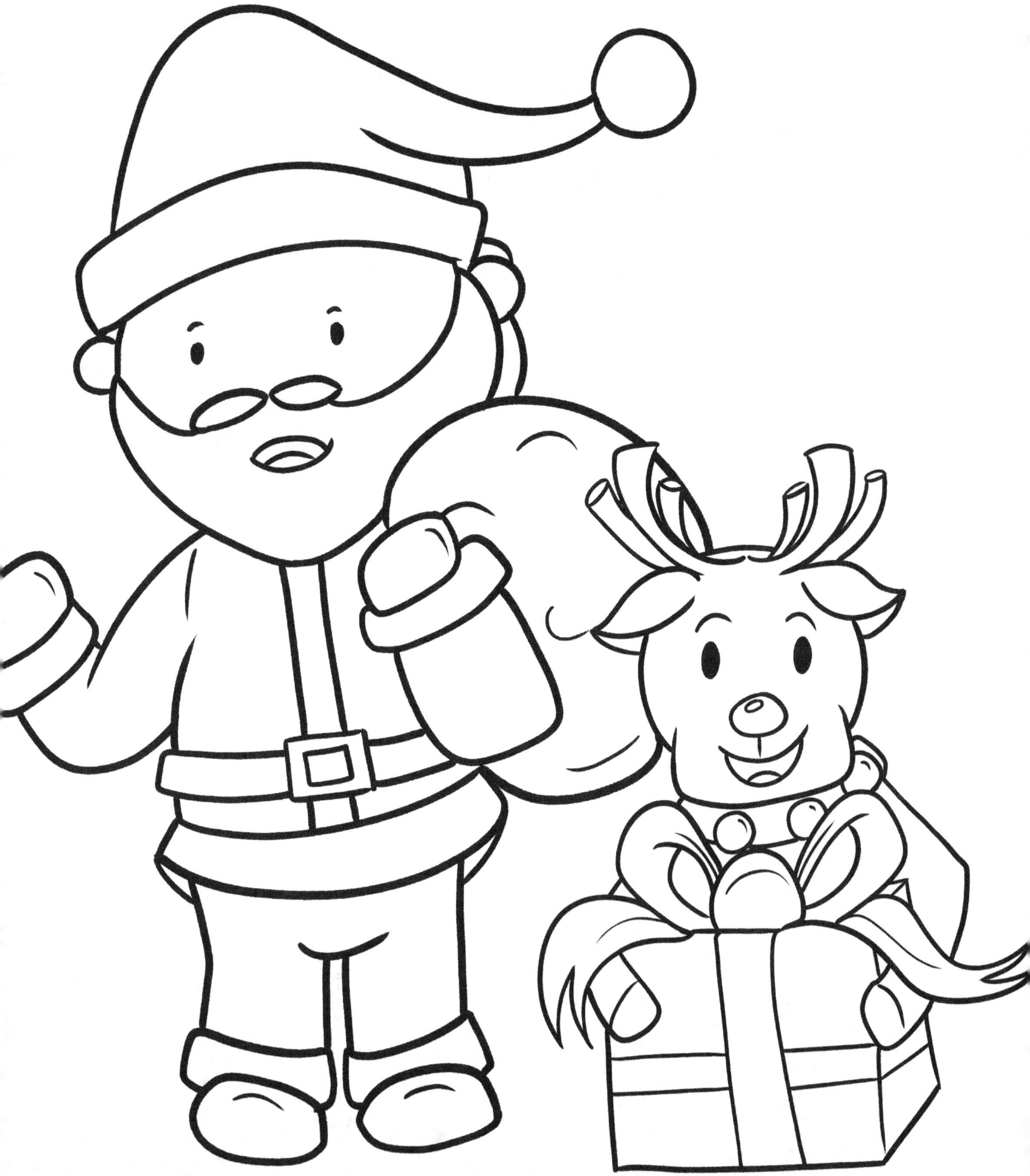

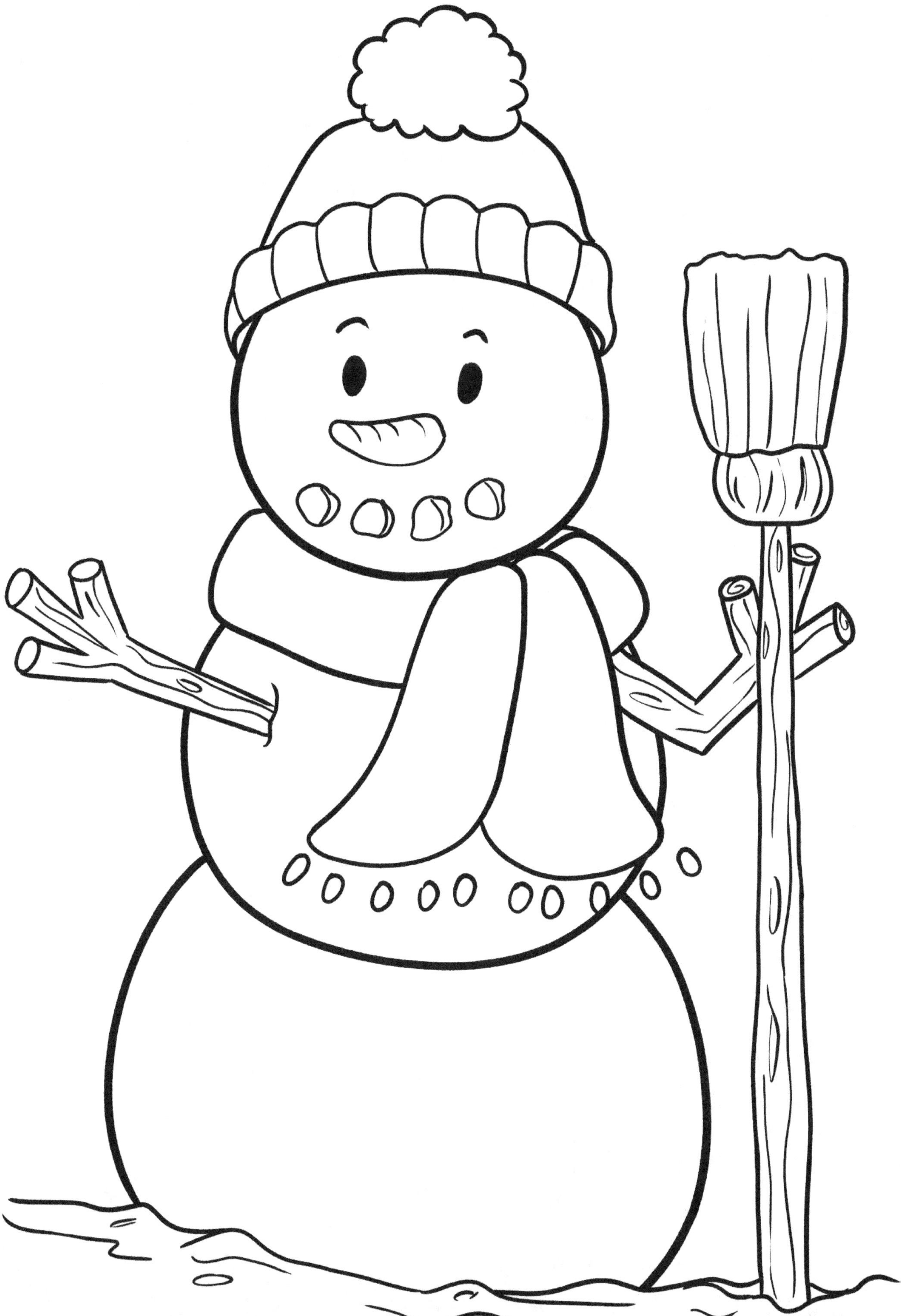

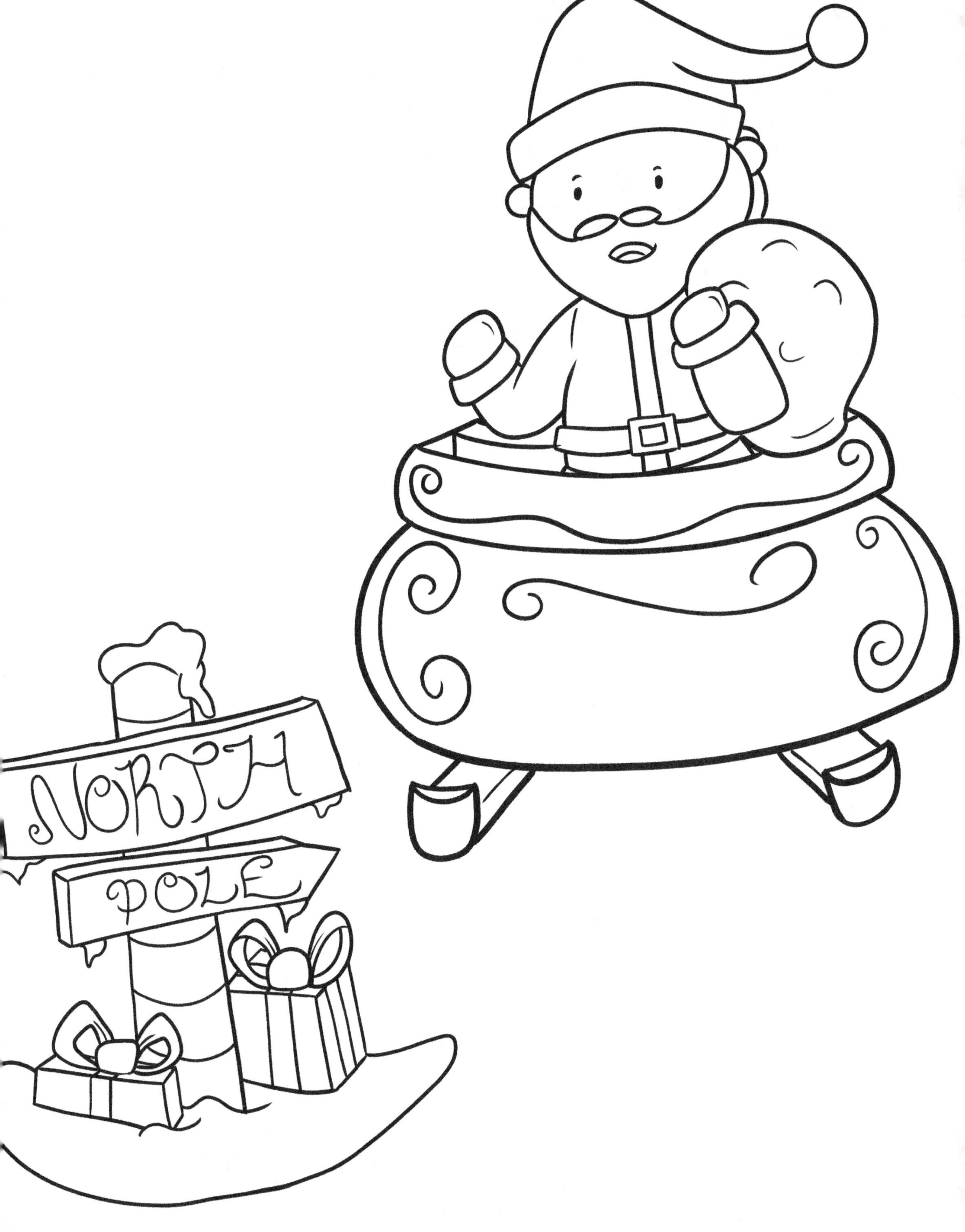
NORTH
POLE

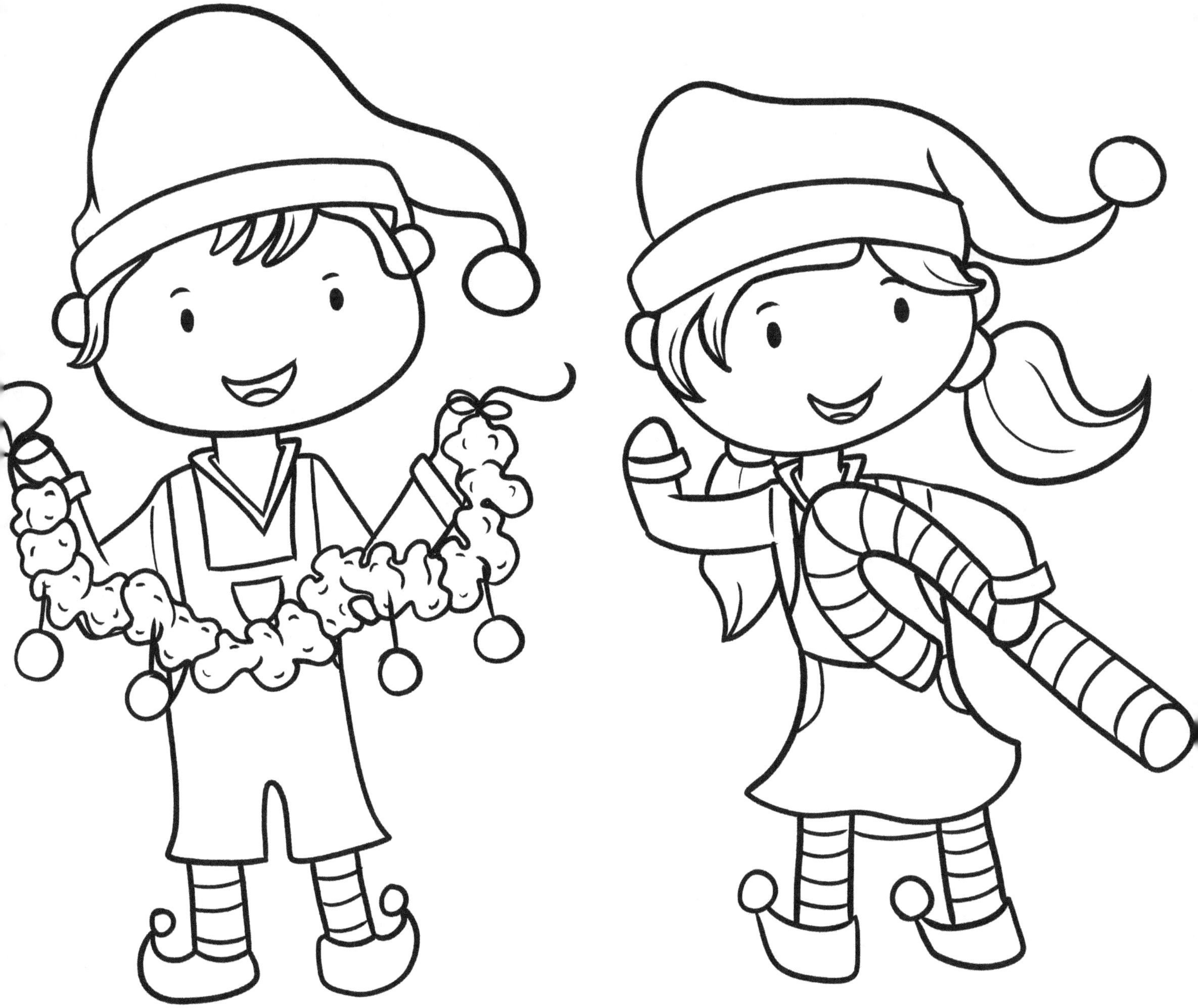

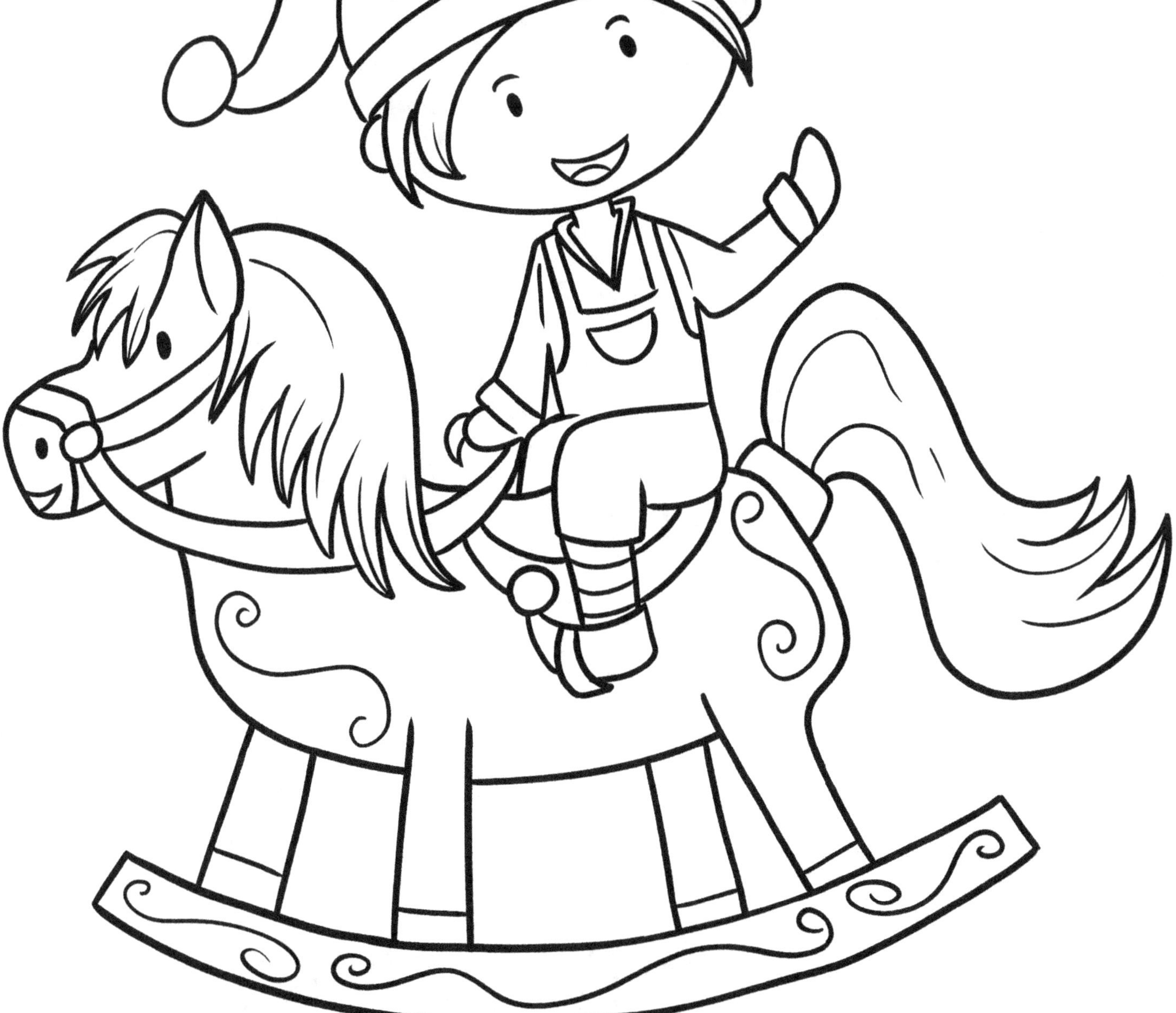

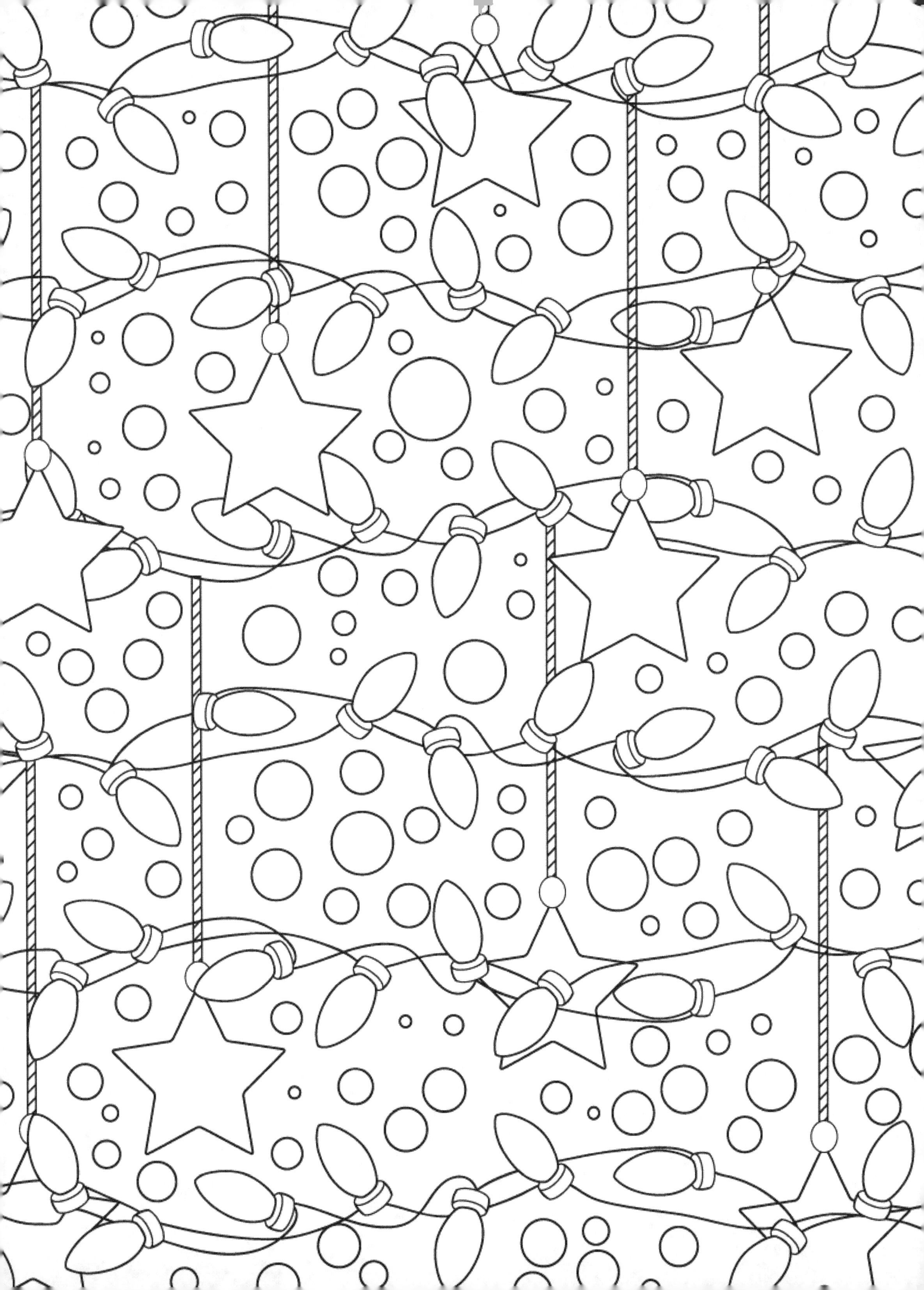

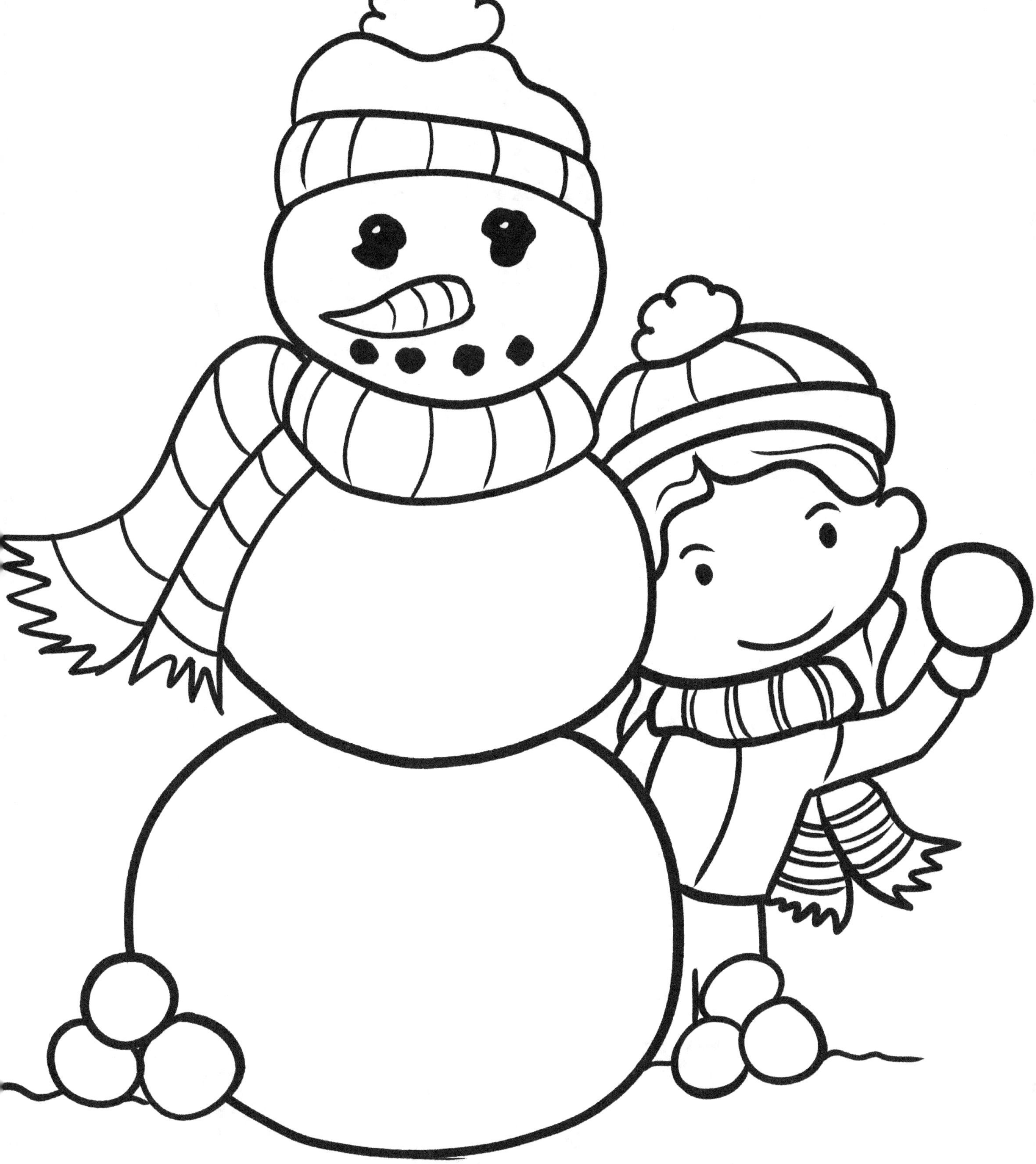

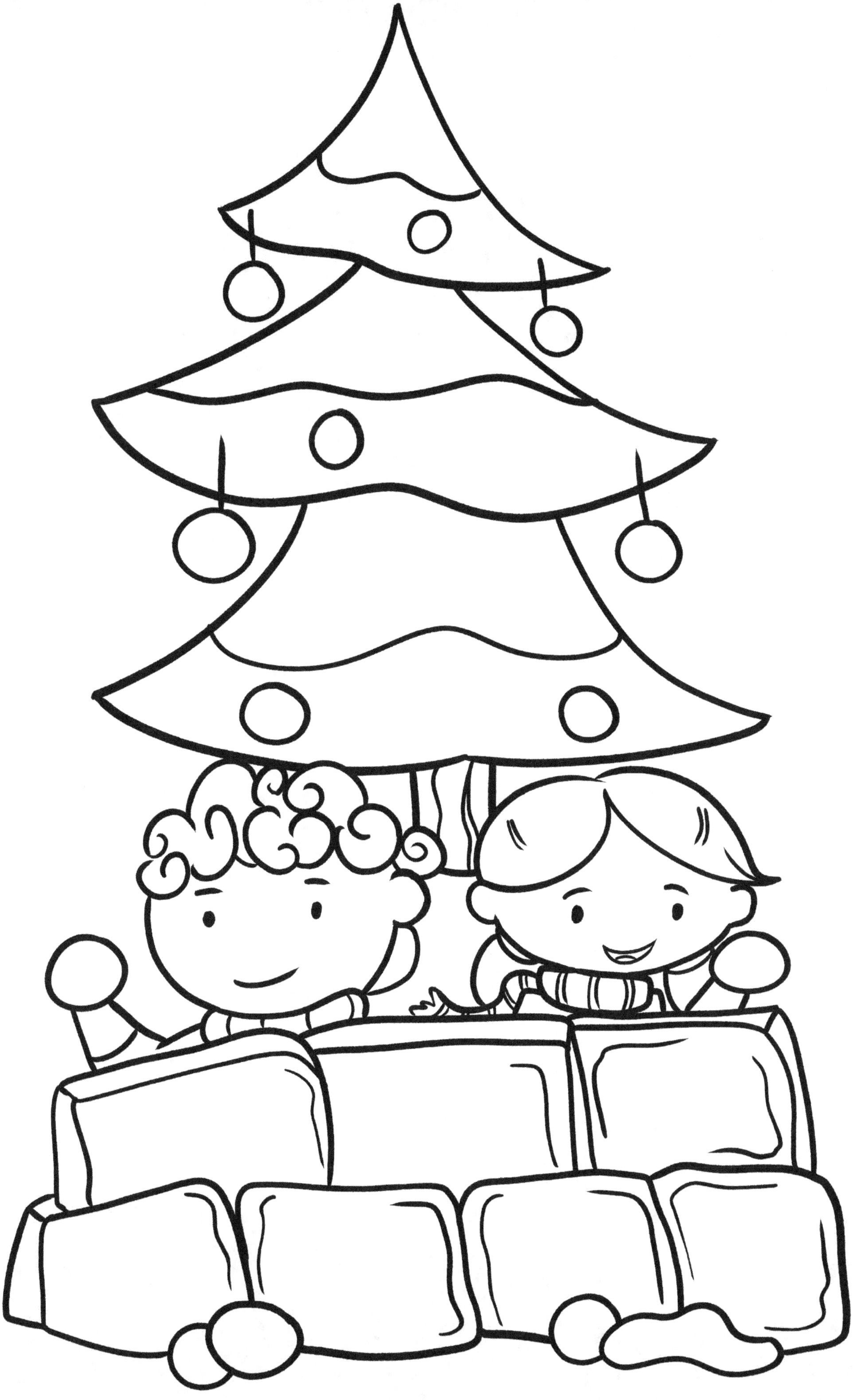

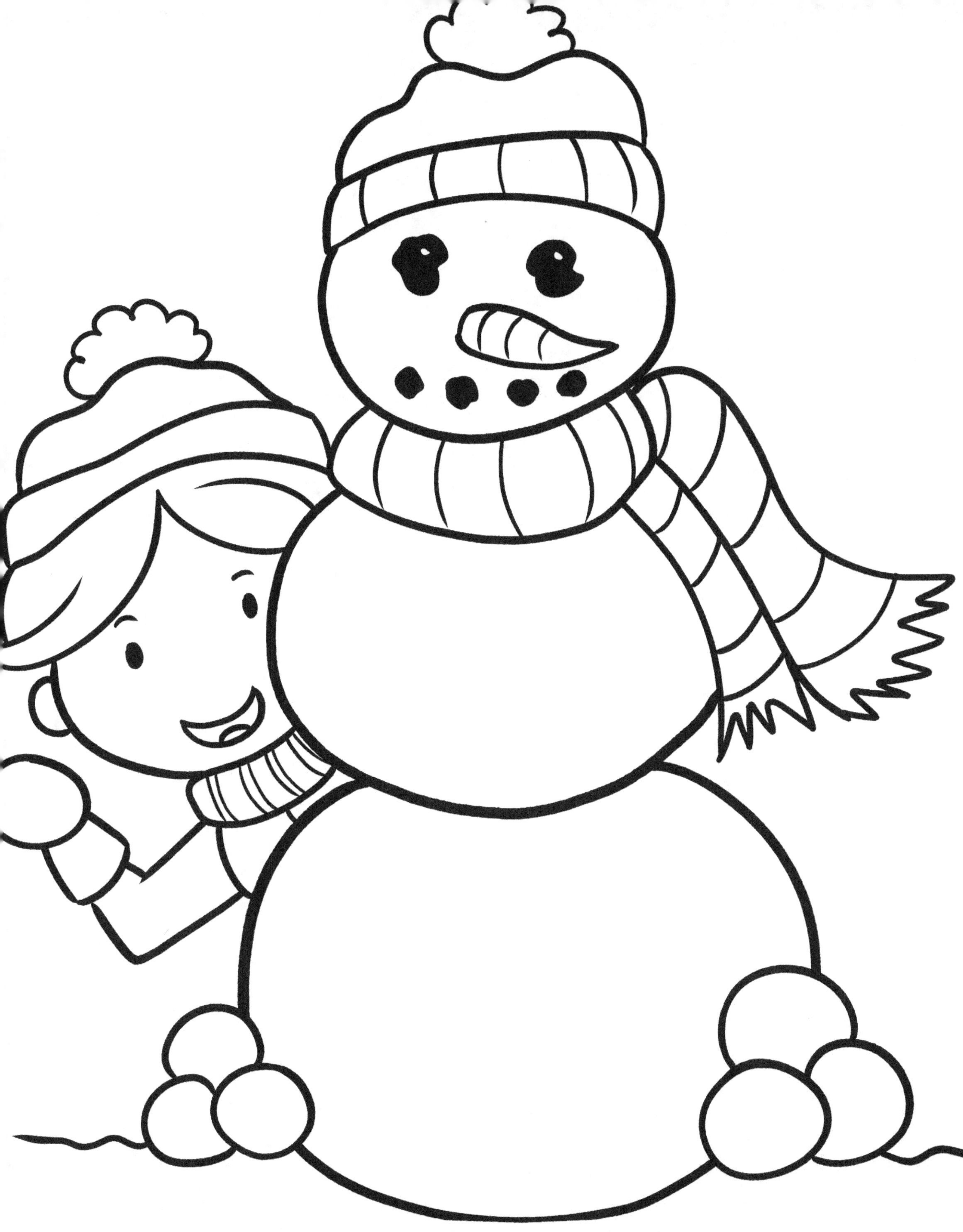

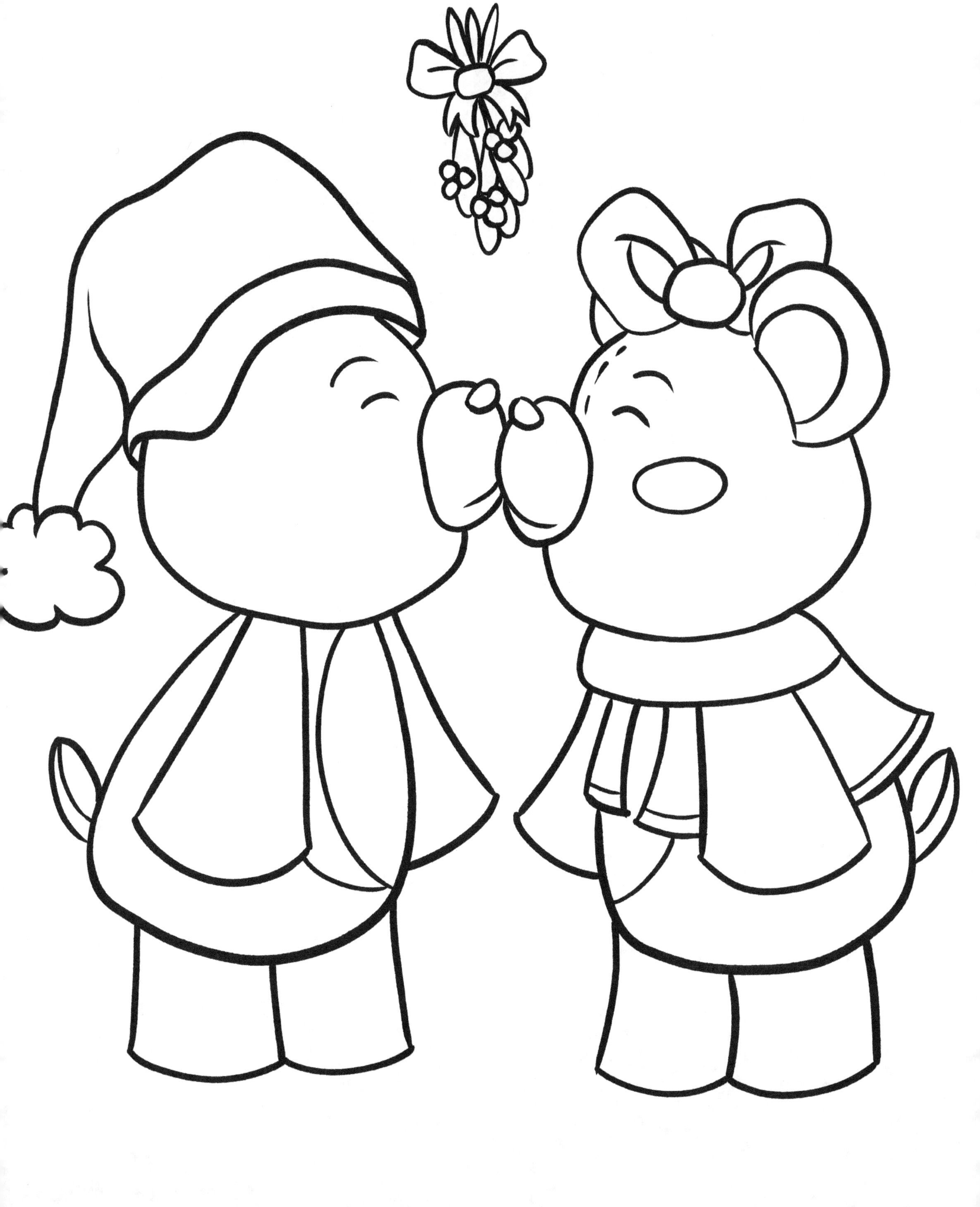

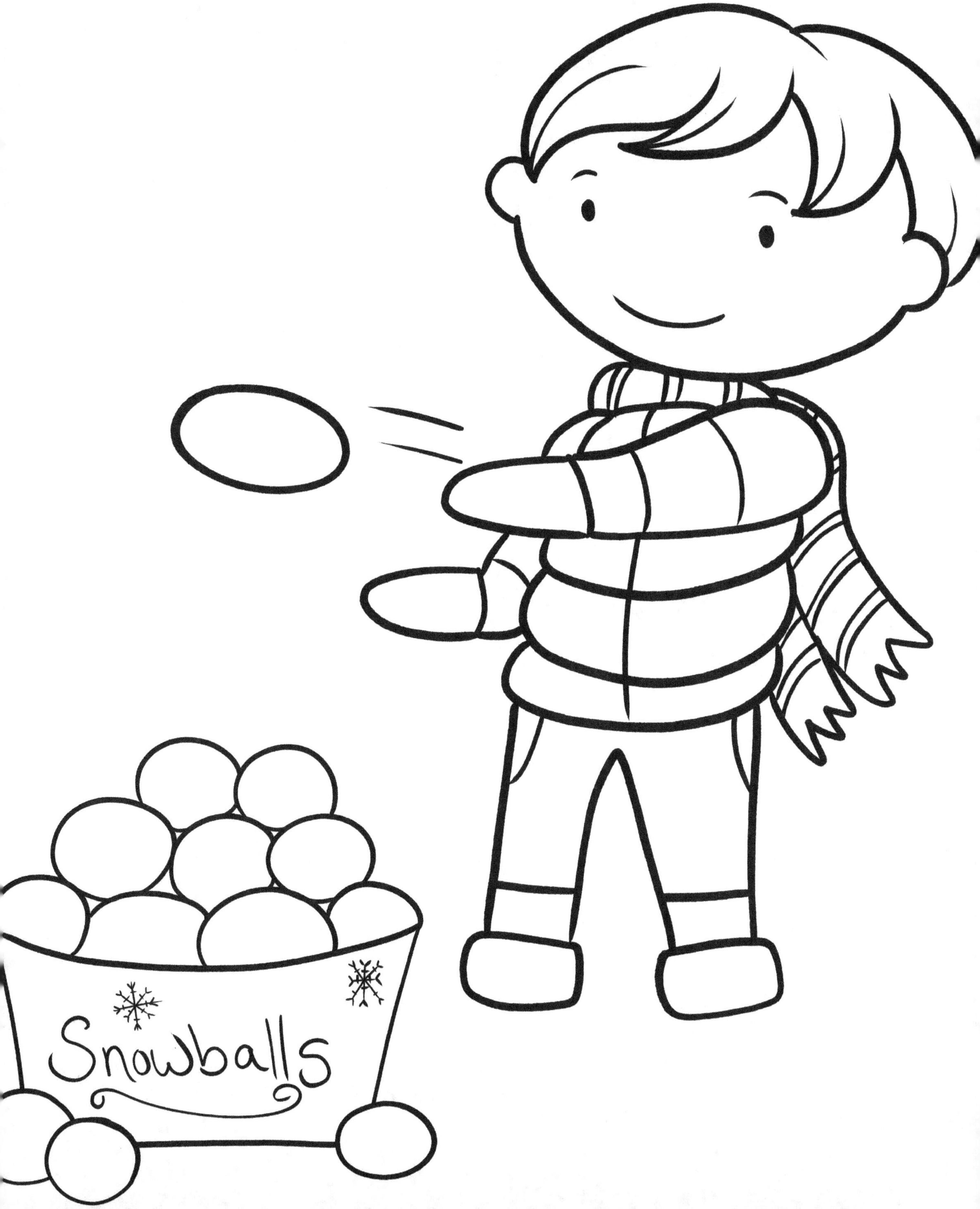
Snowballs

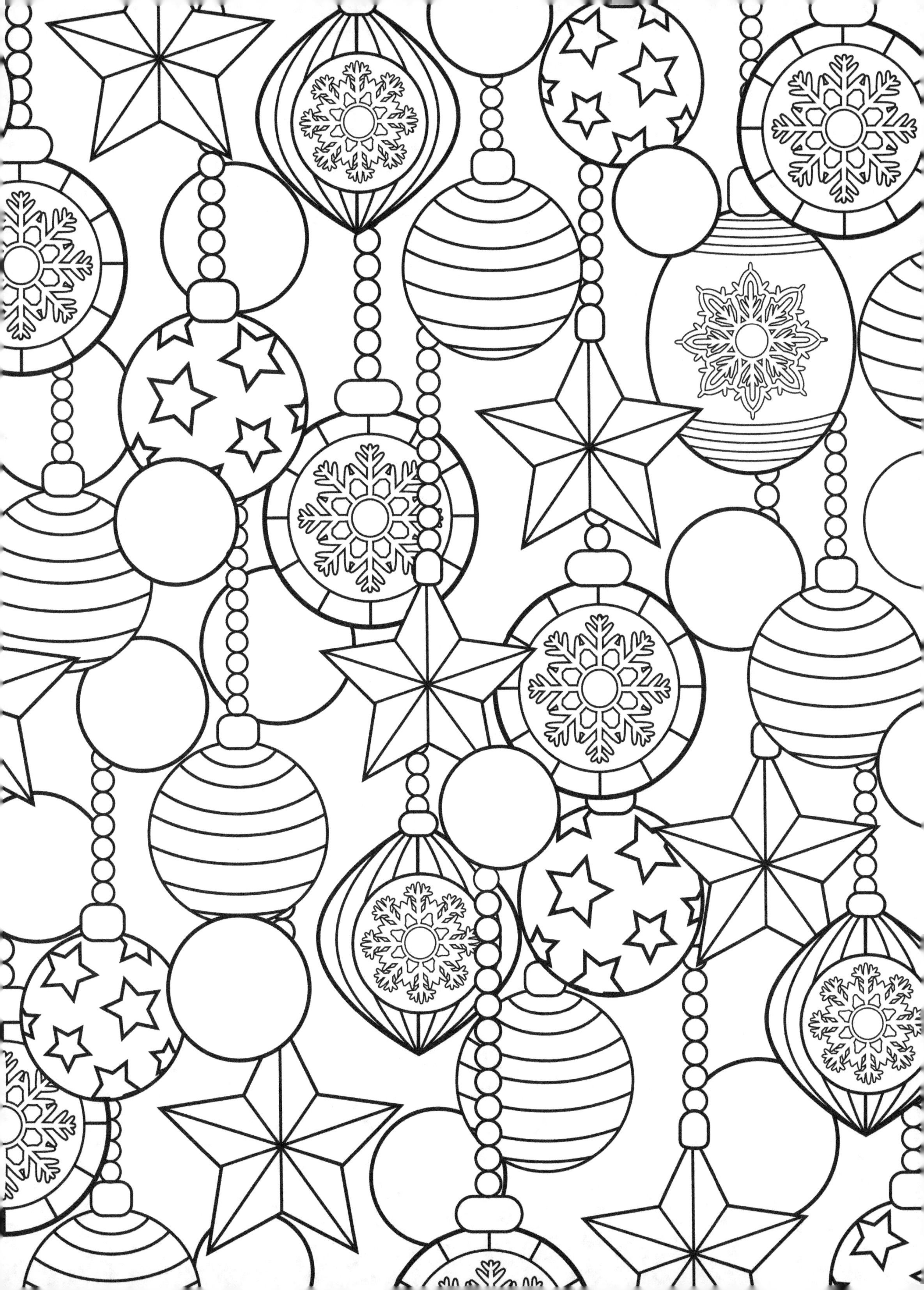

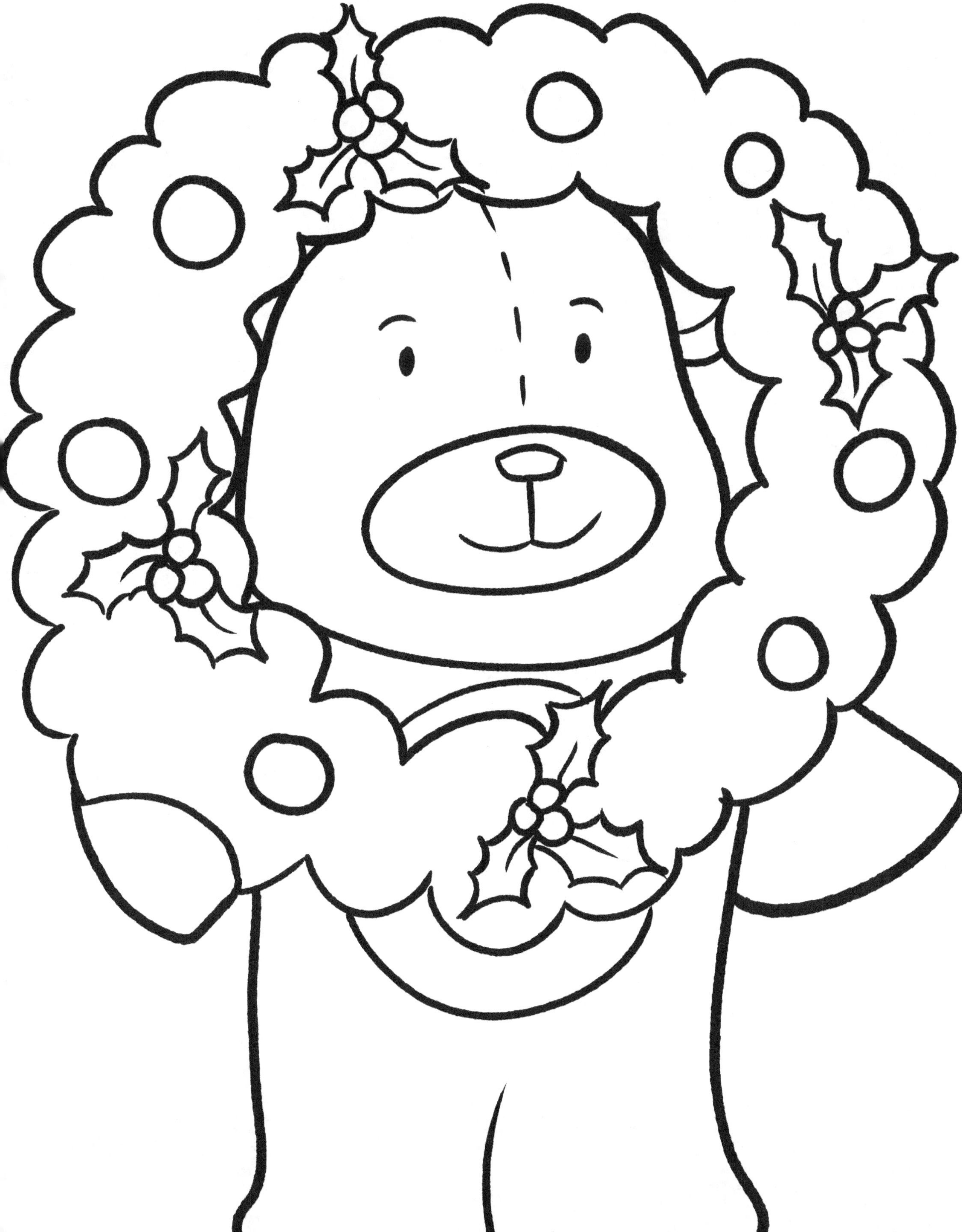

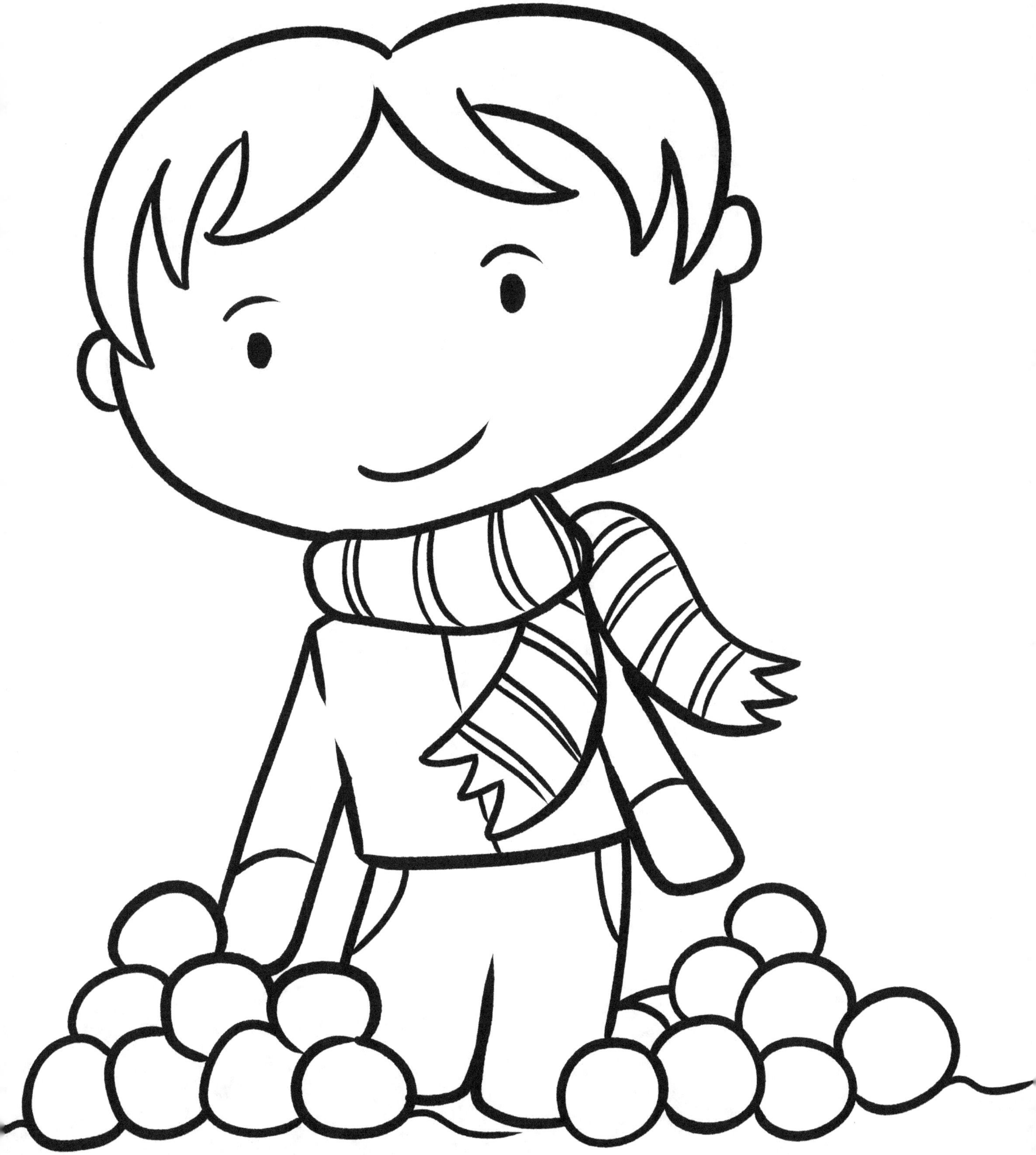

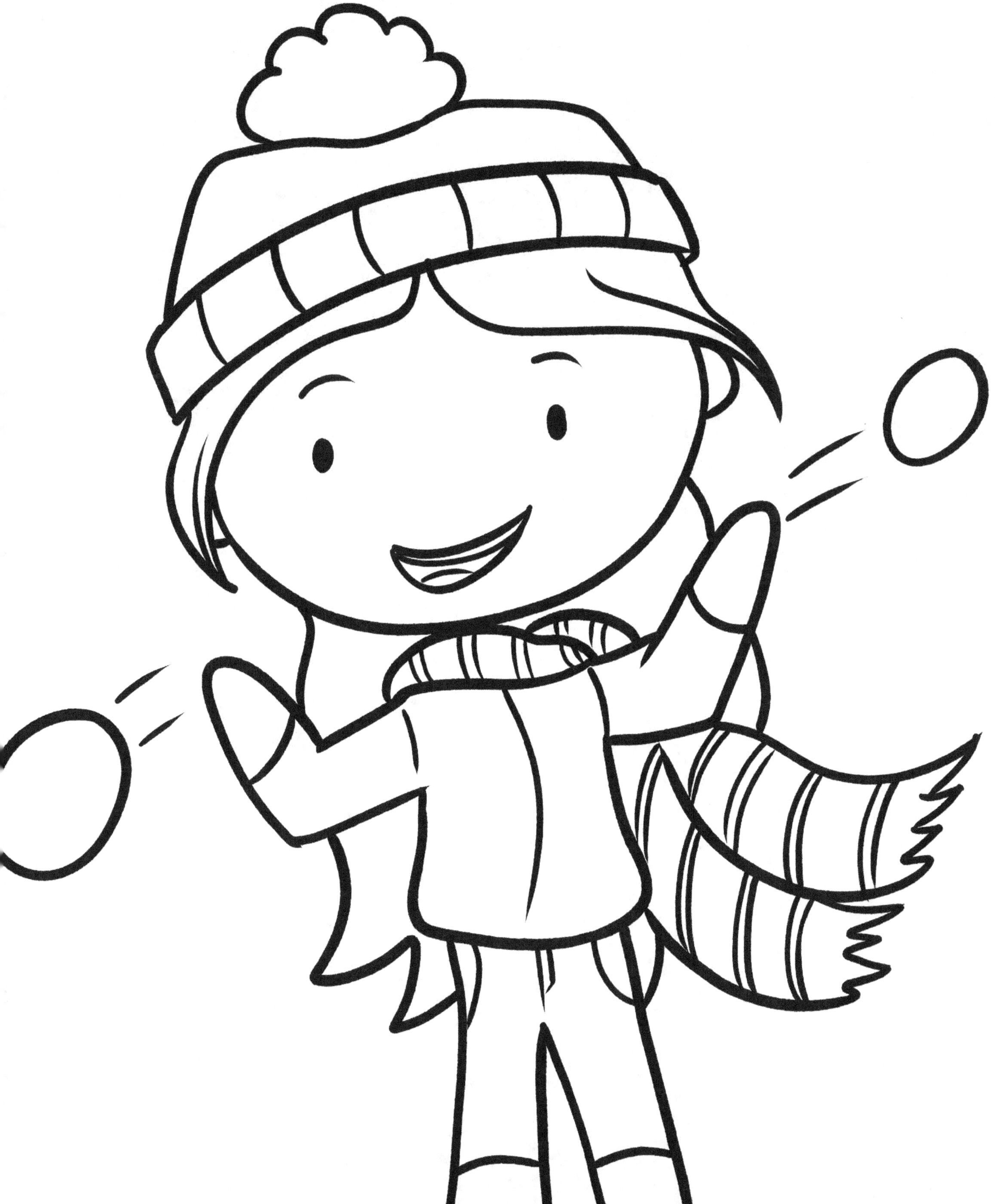

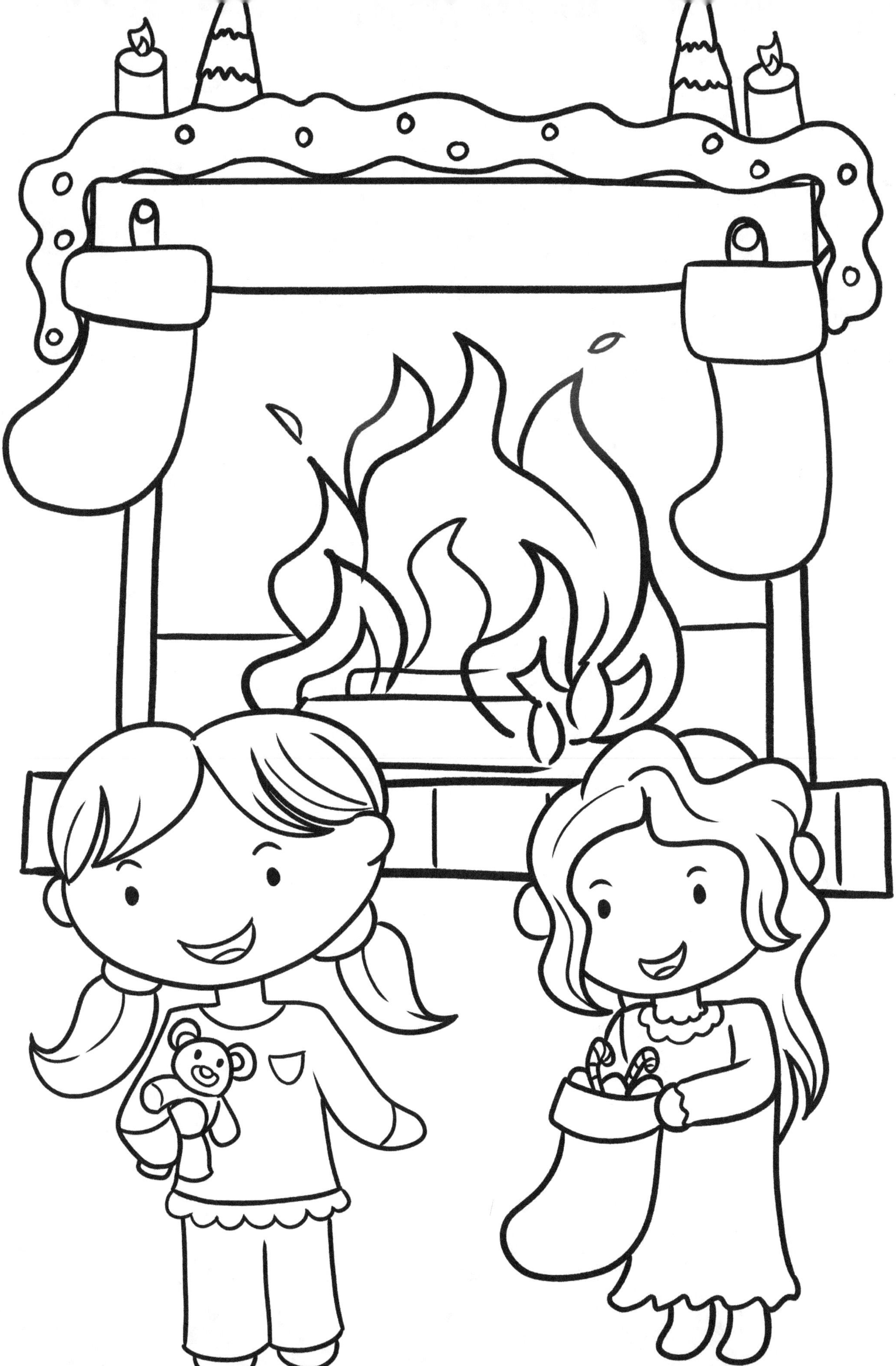

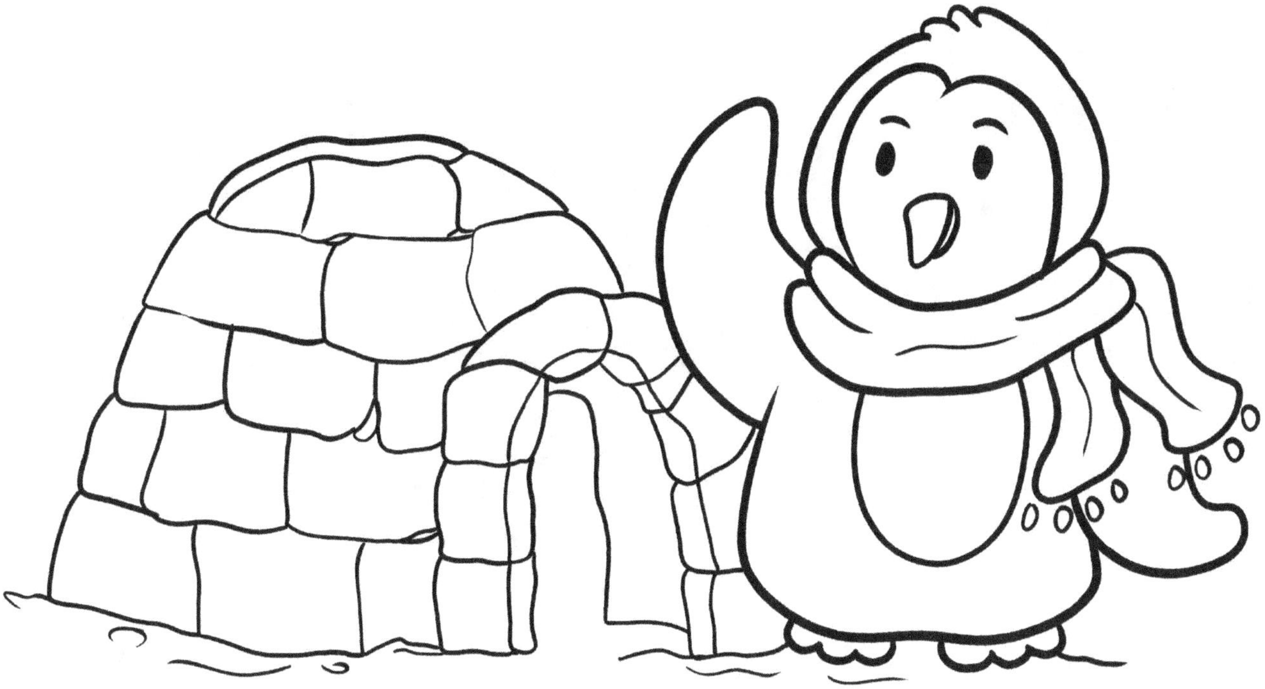

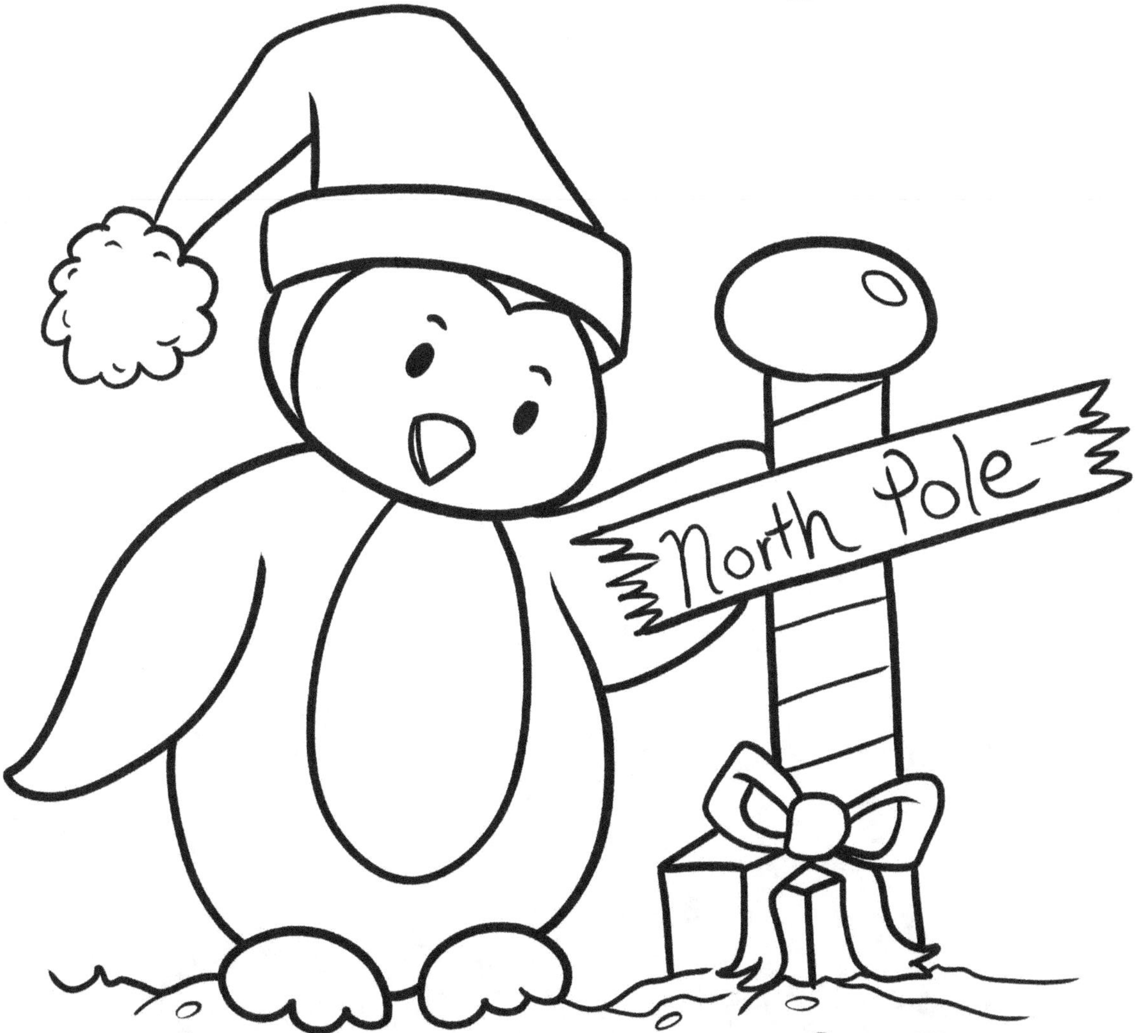
North Pole

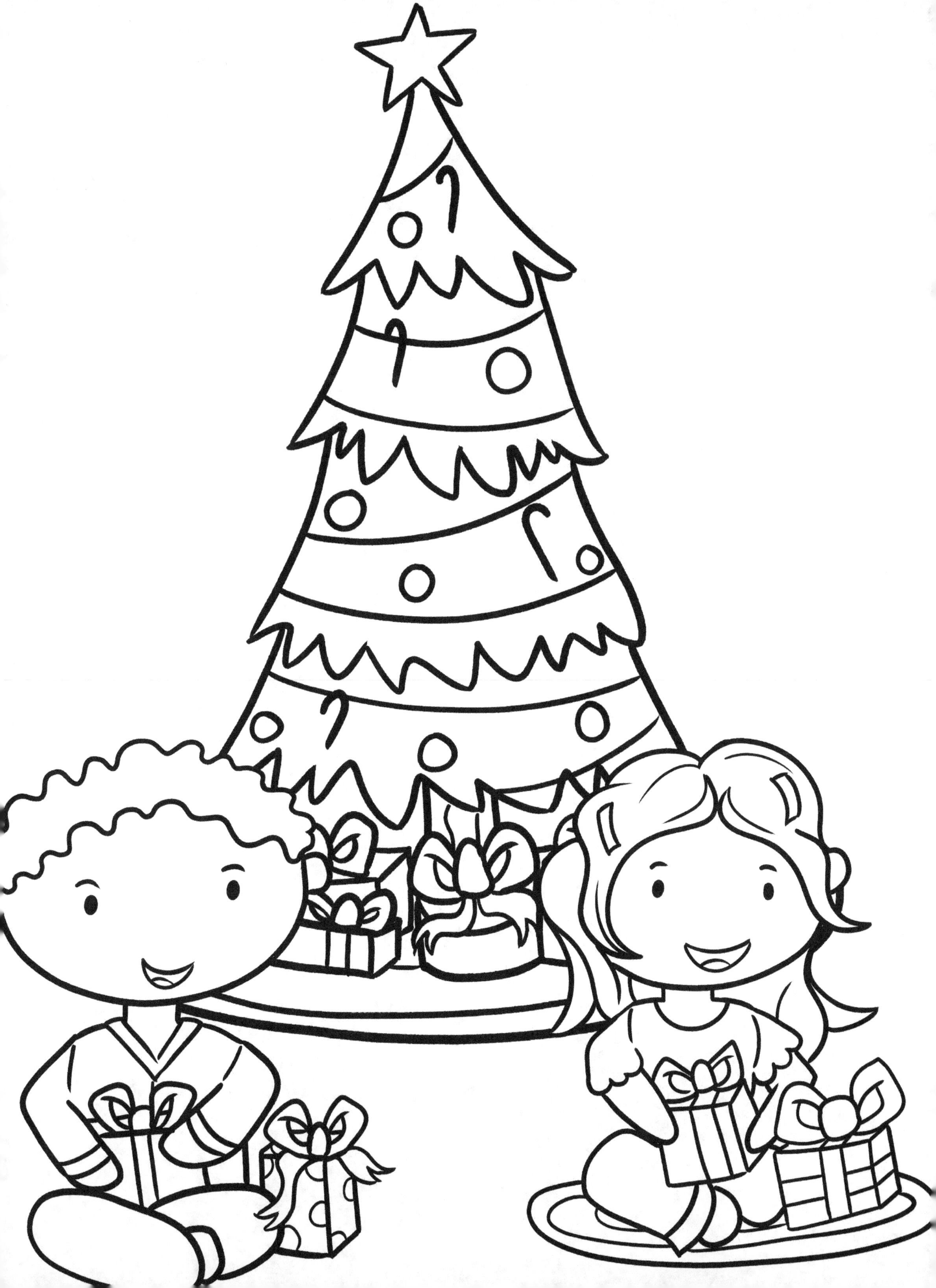

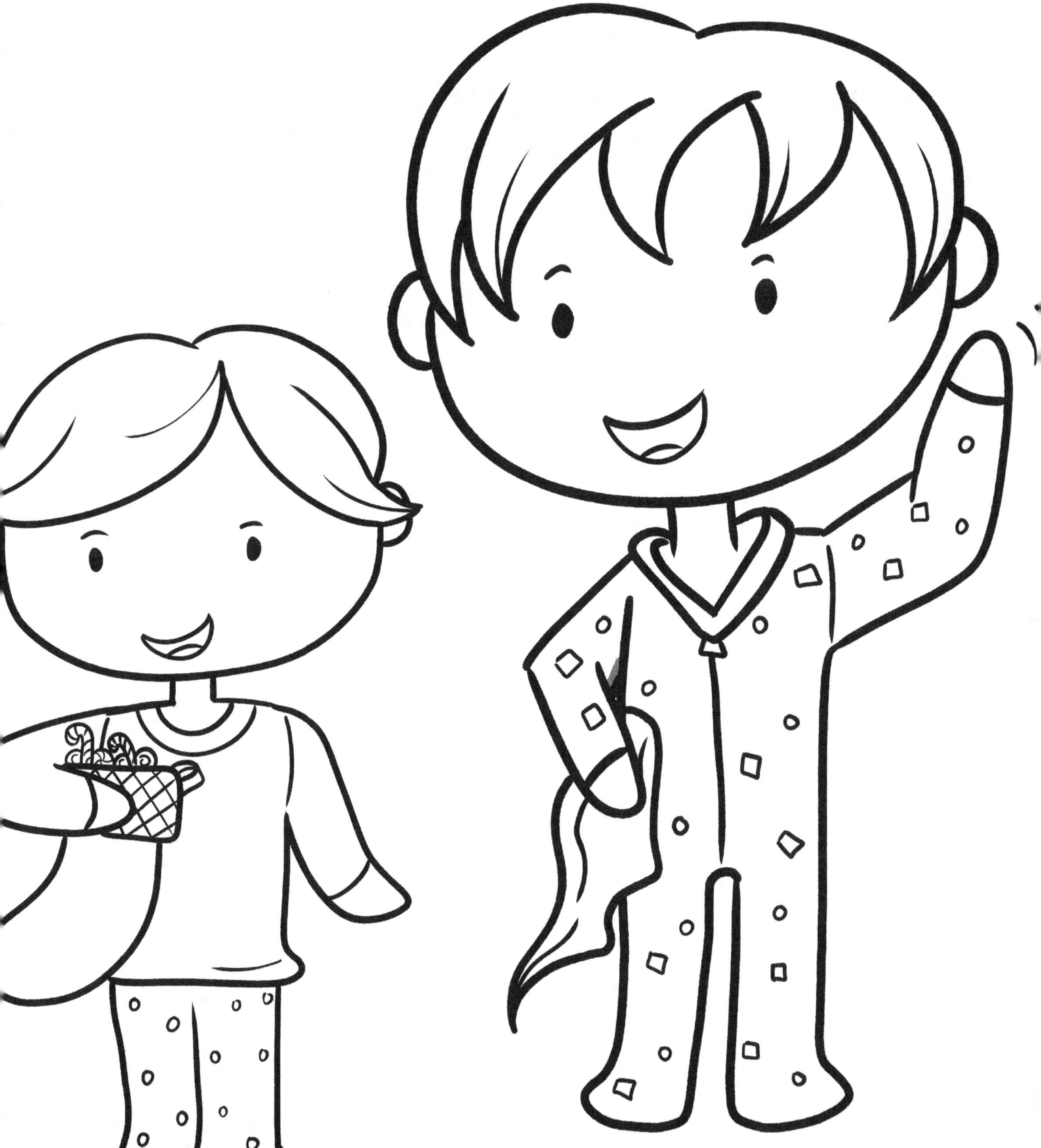

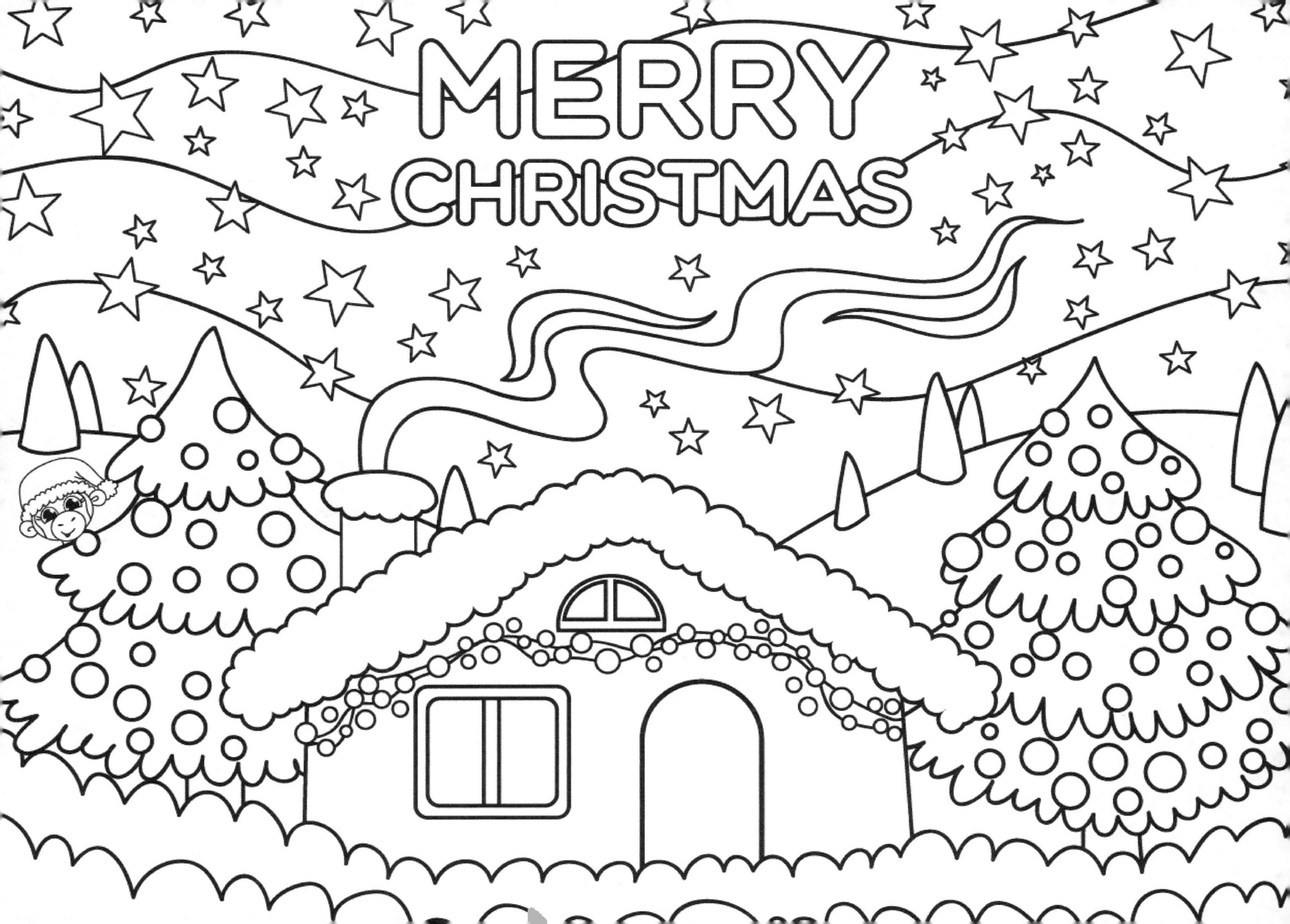
MERRY CHRISTMAS

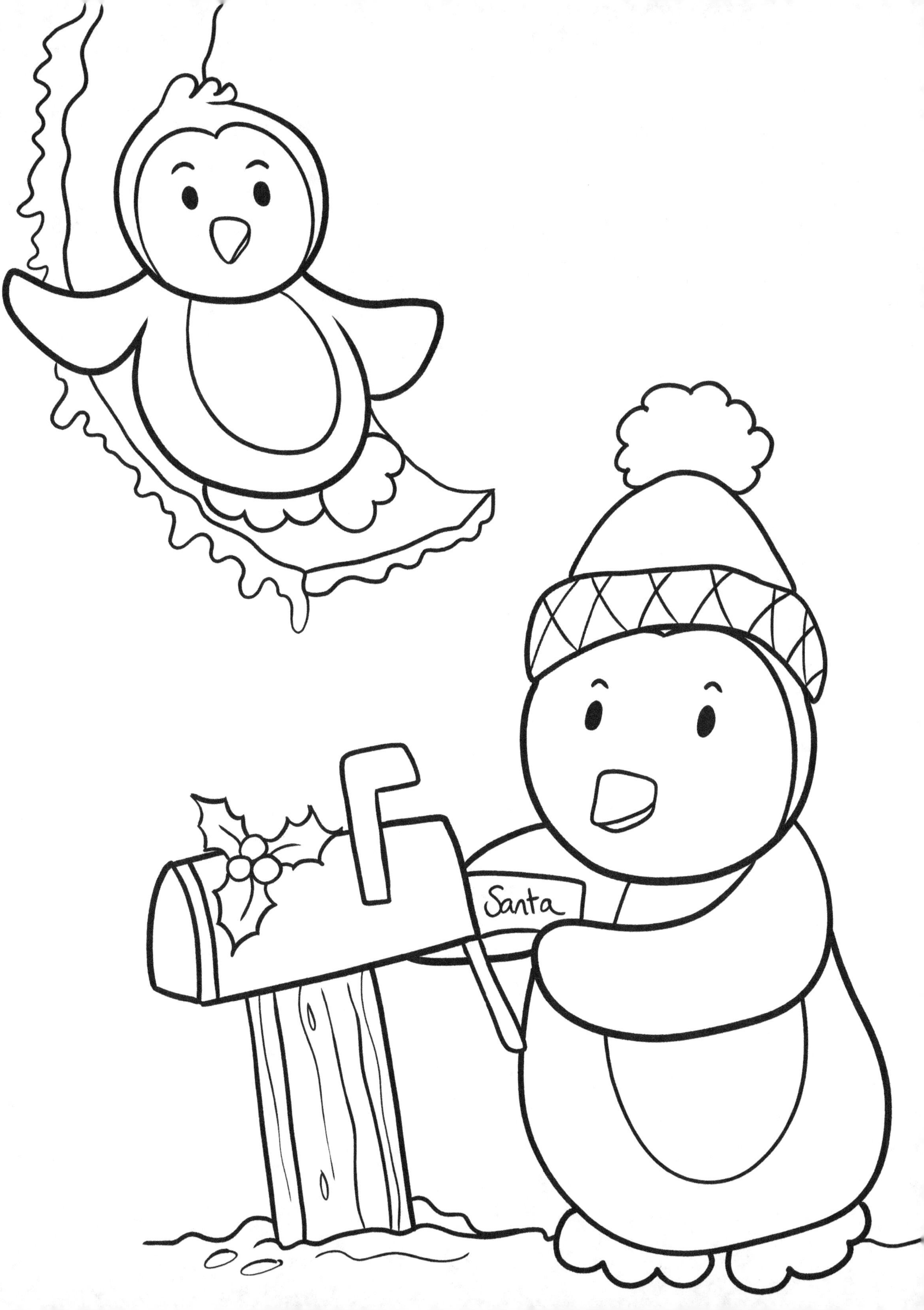
Santa

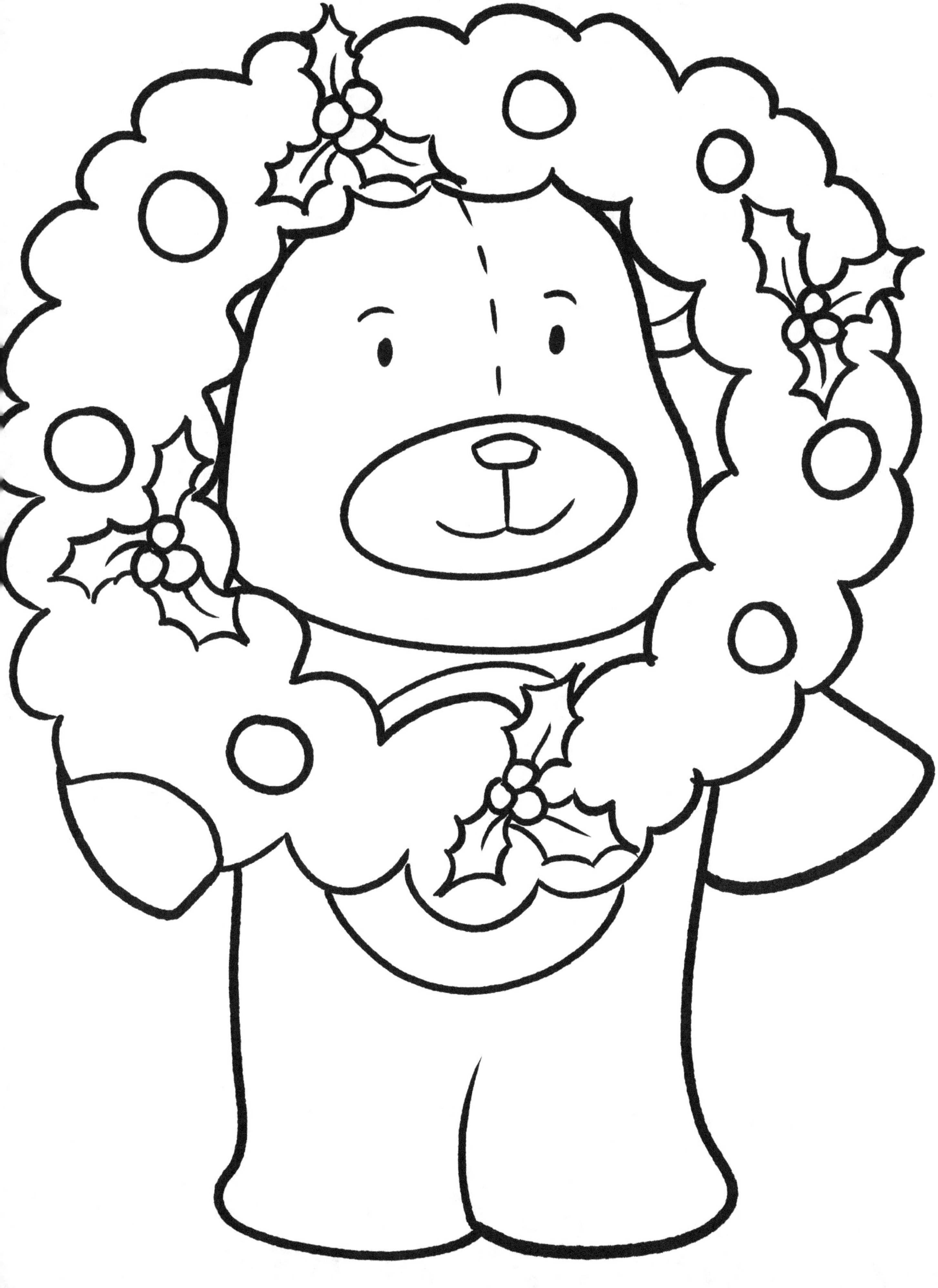

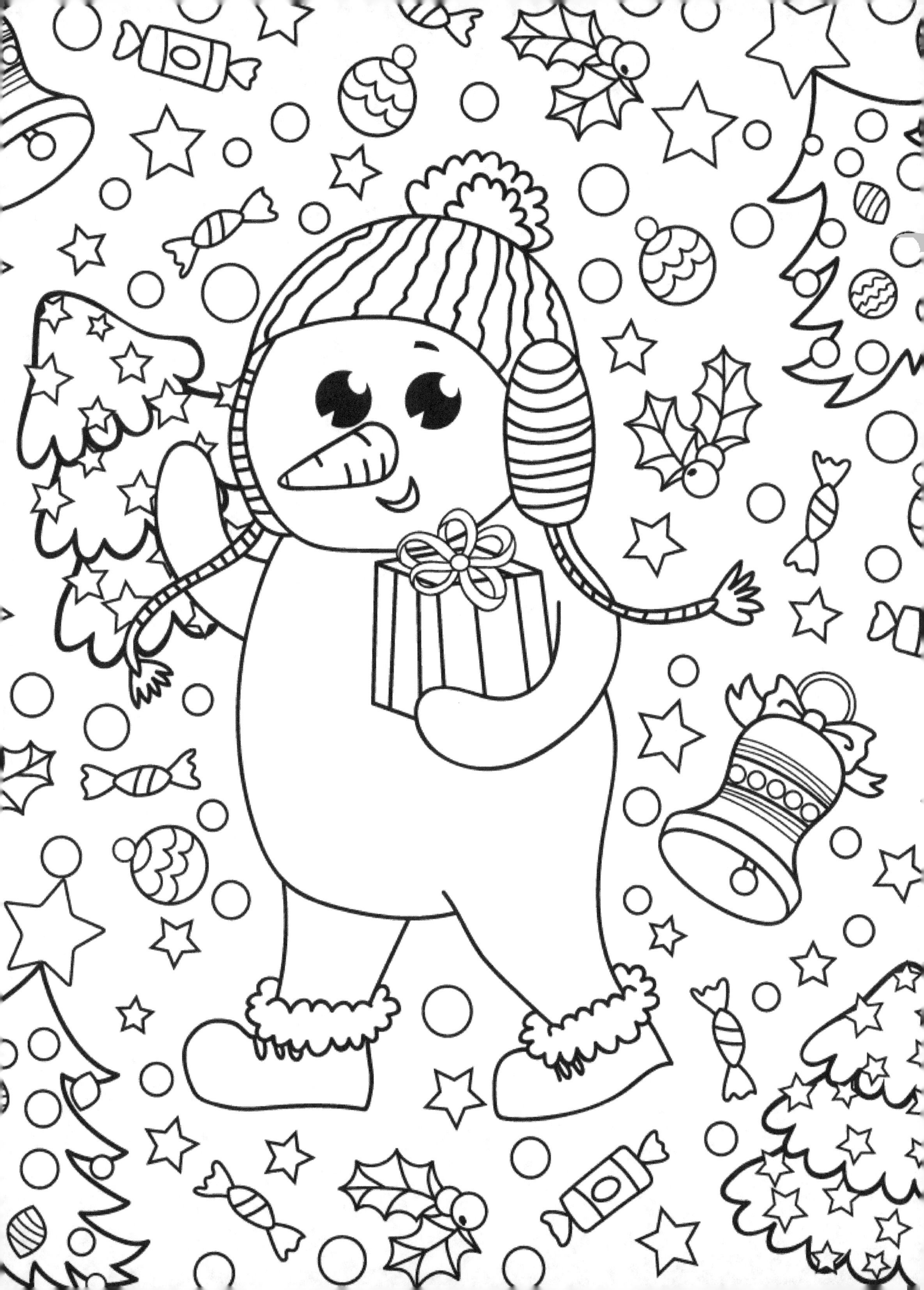

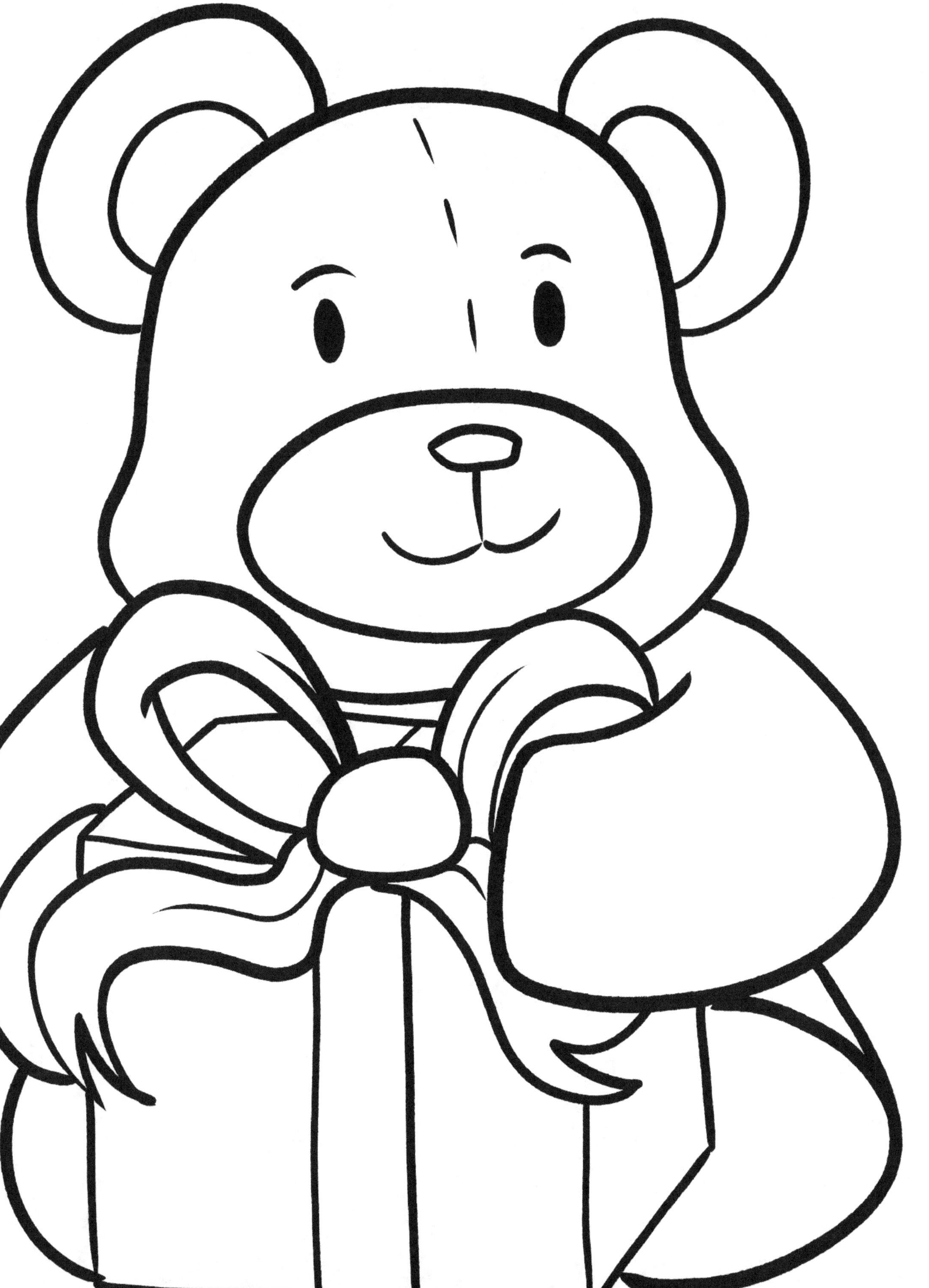

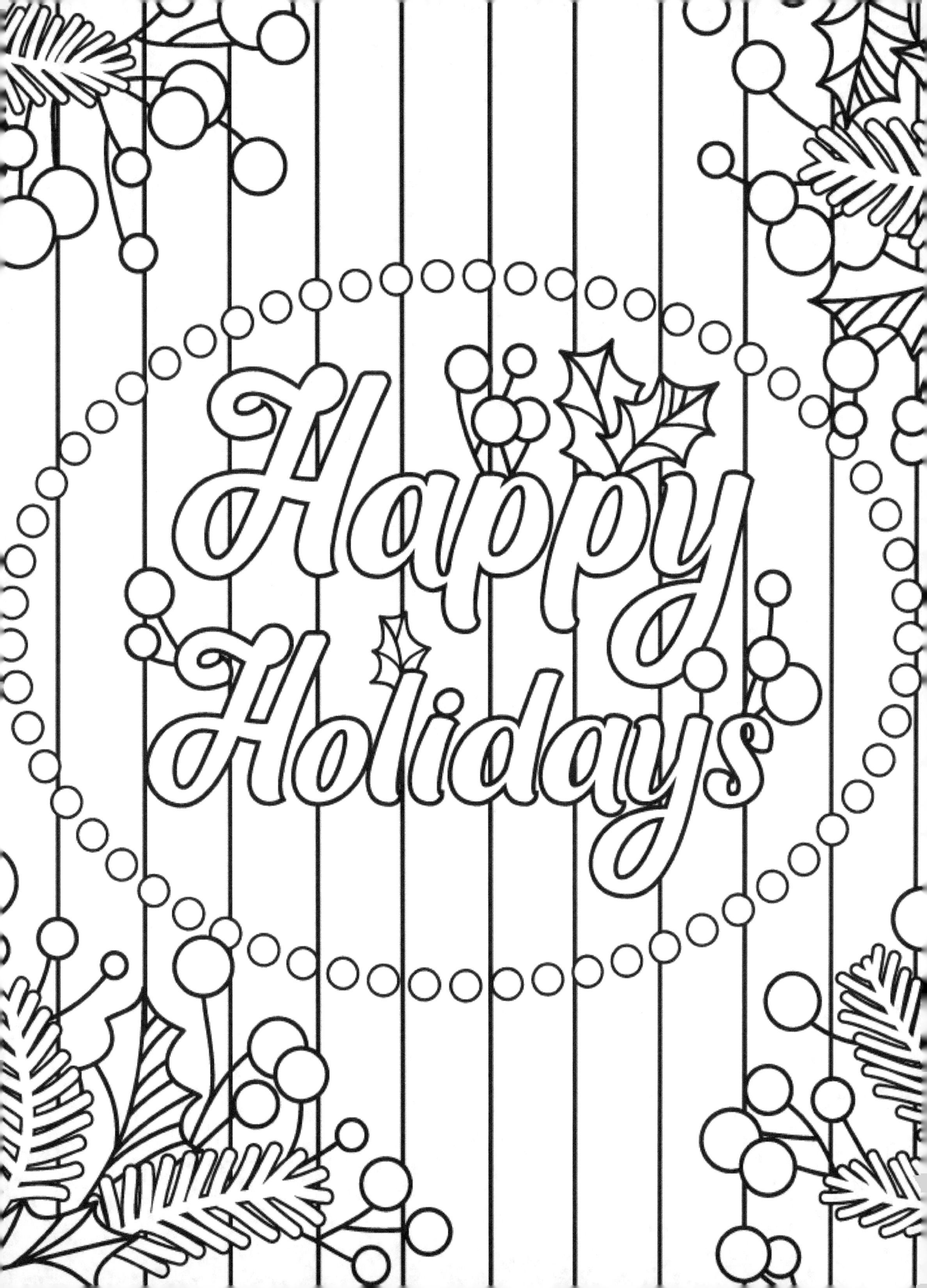
Happy Holidays

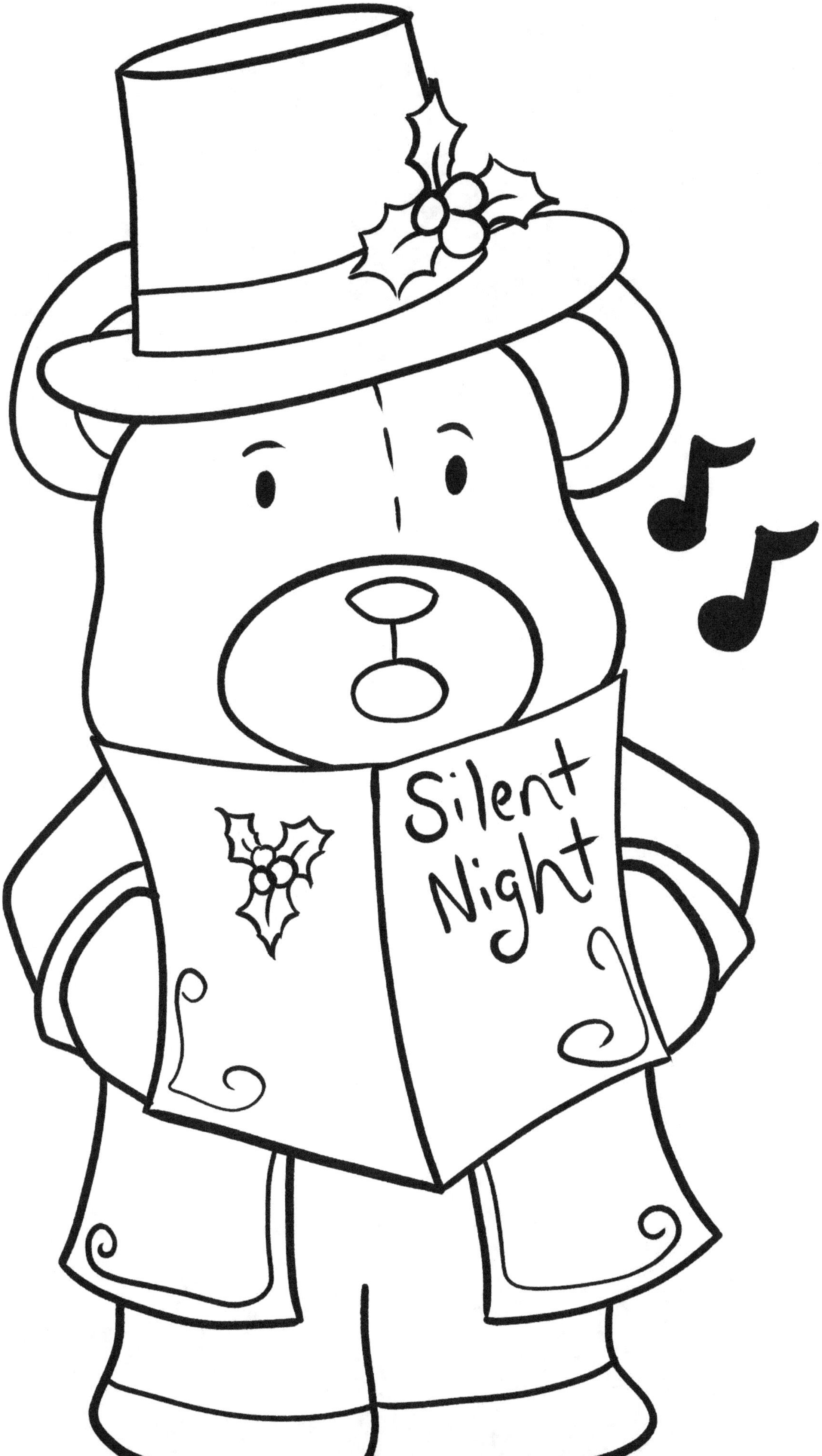
Silent Night

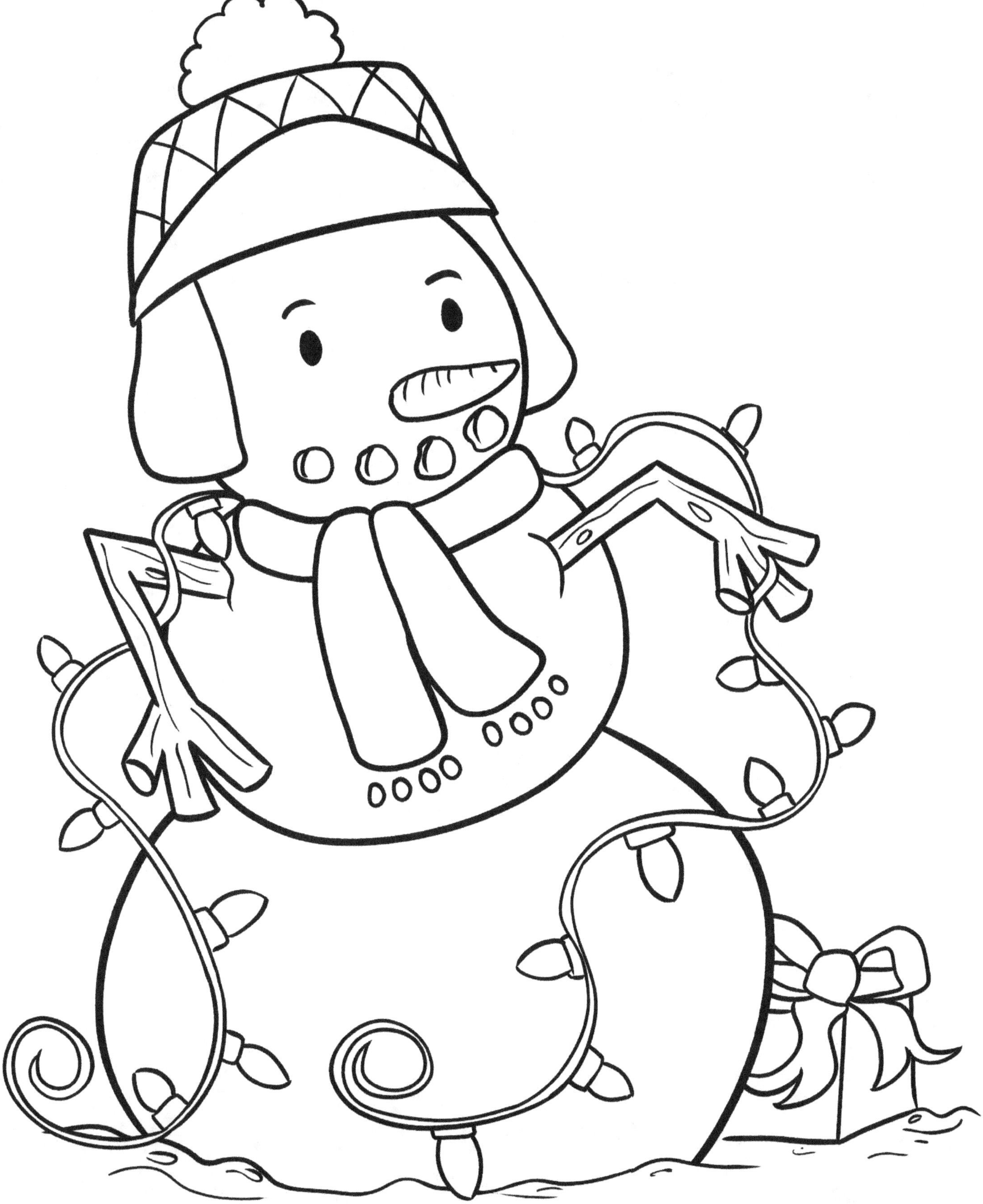

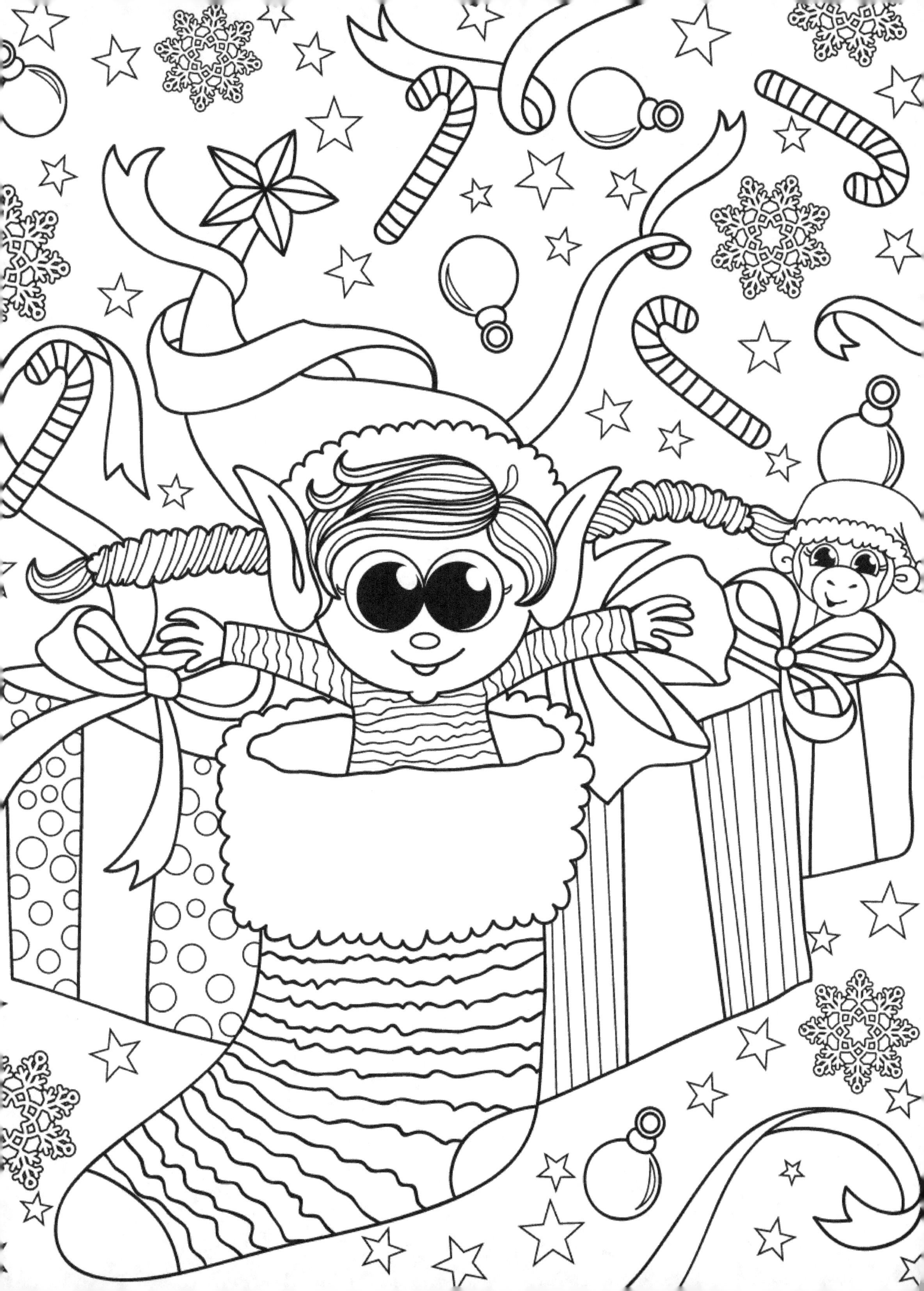

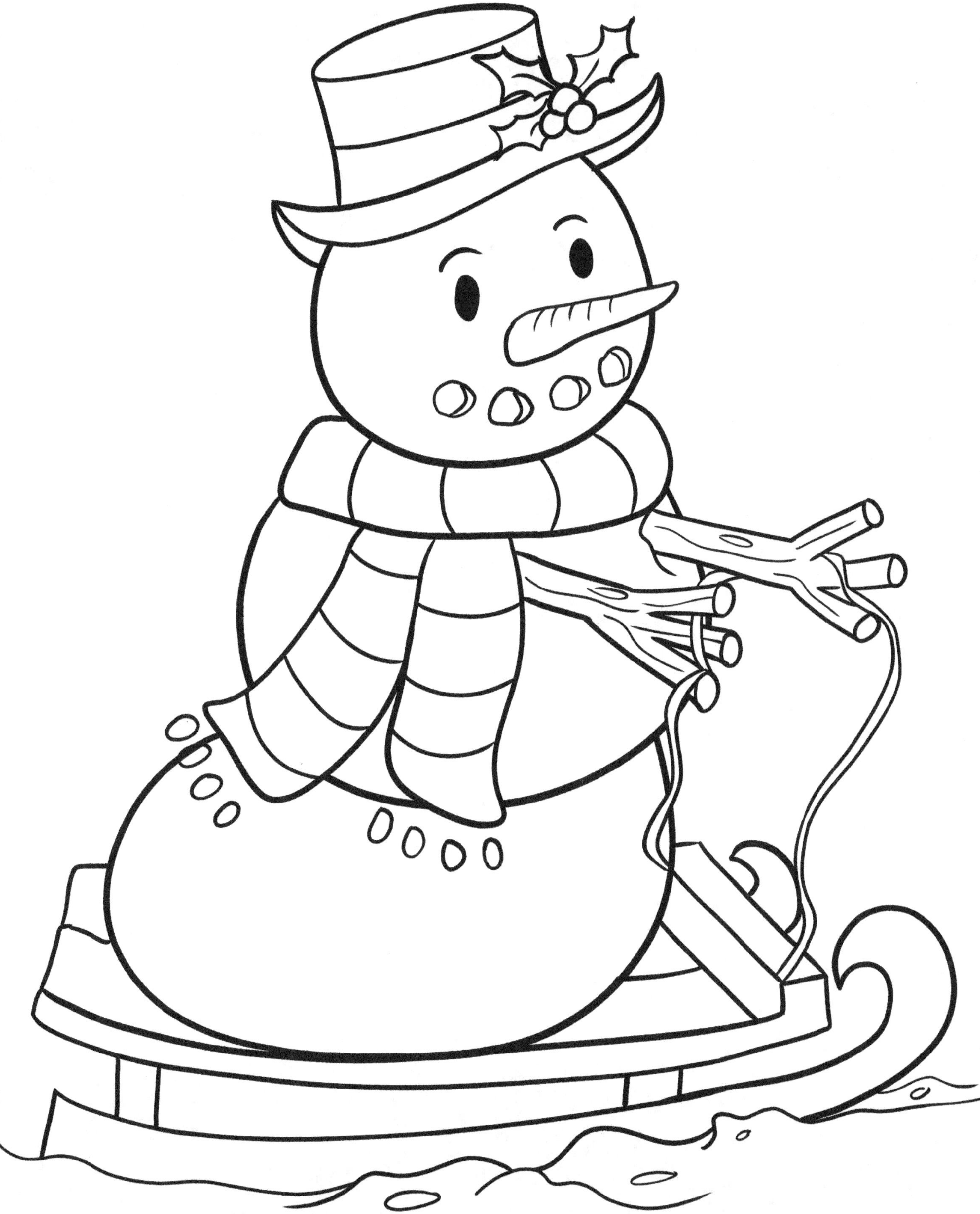

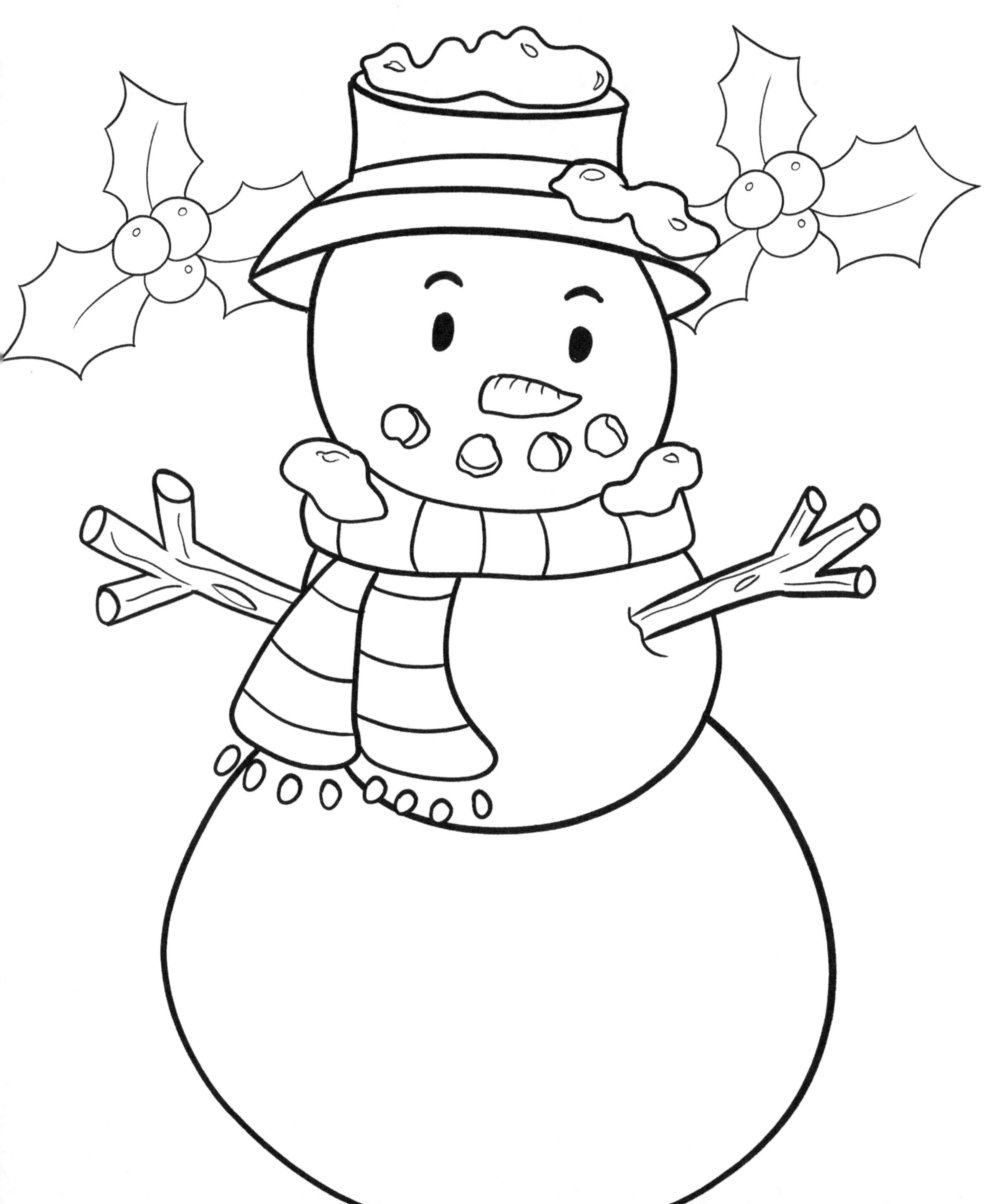

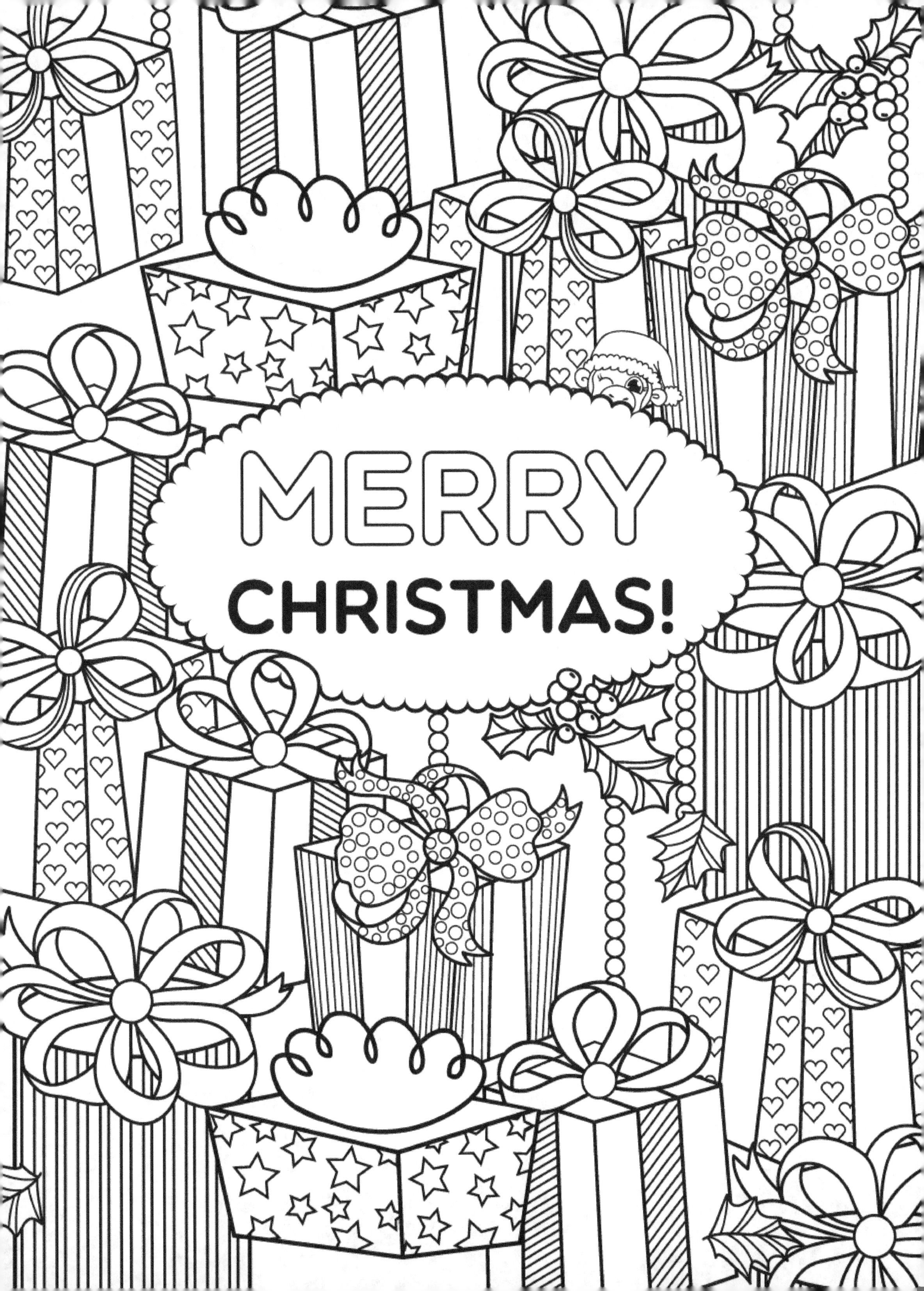
MERRY
CHRISTMAS!

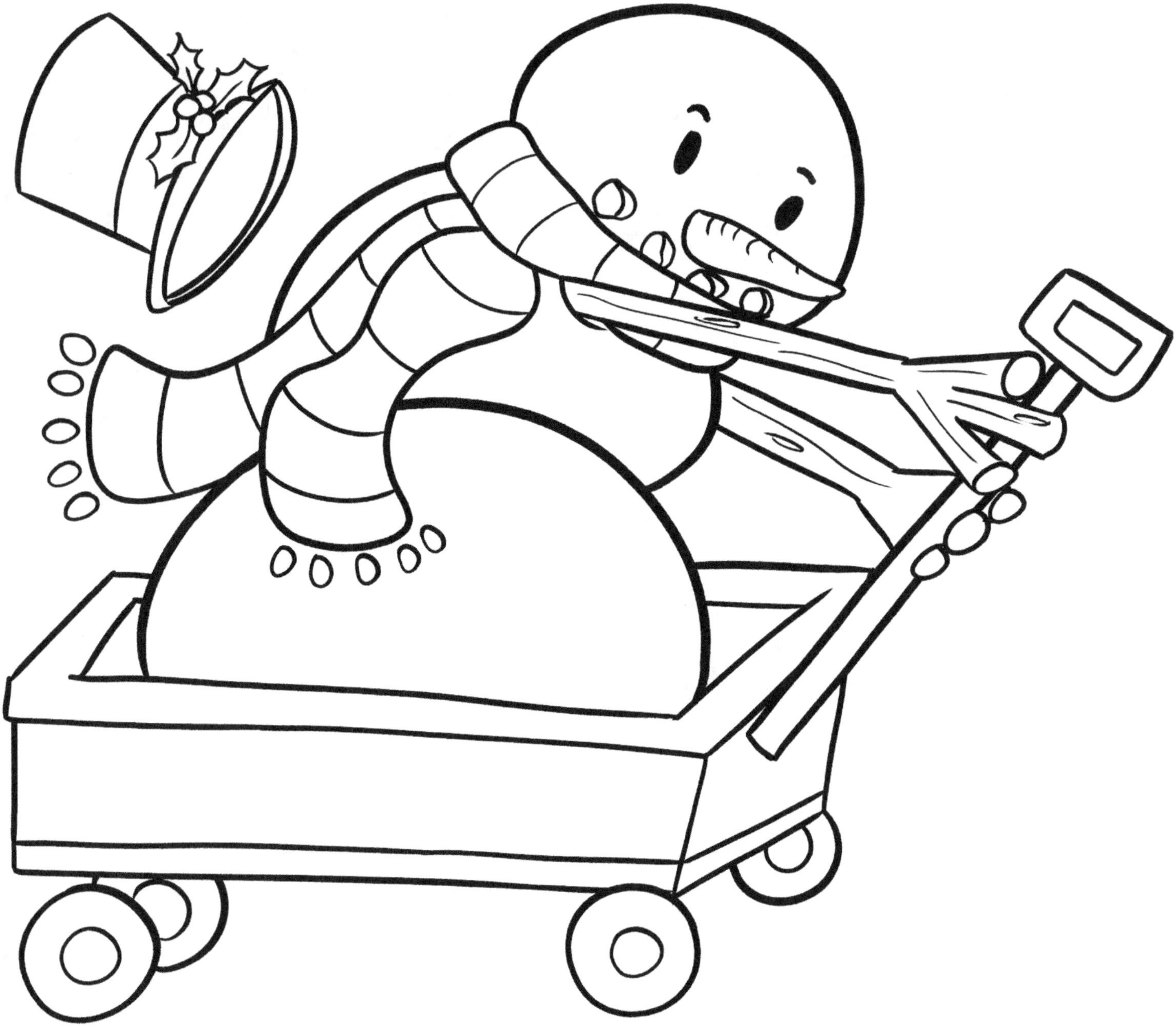

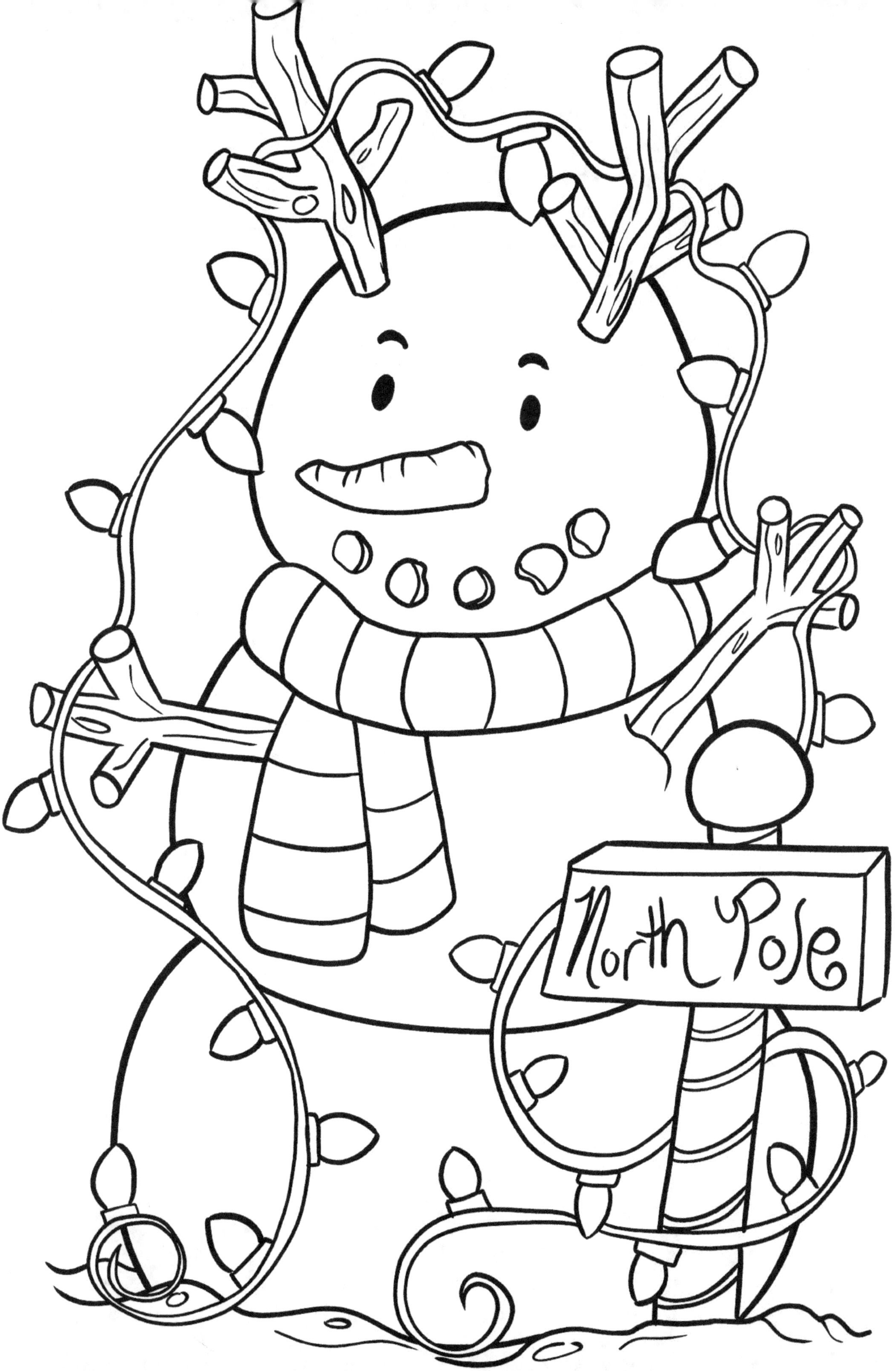
North Pole

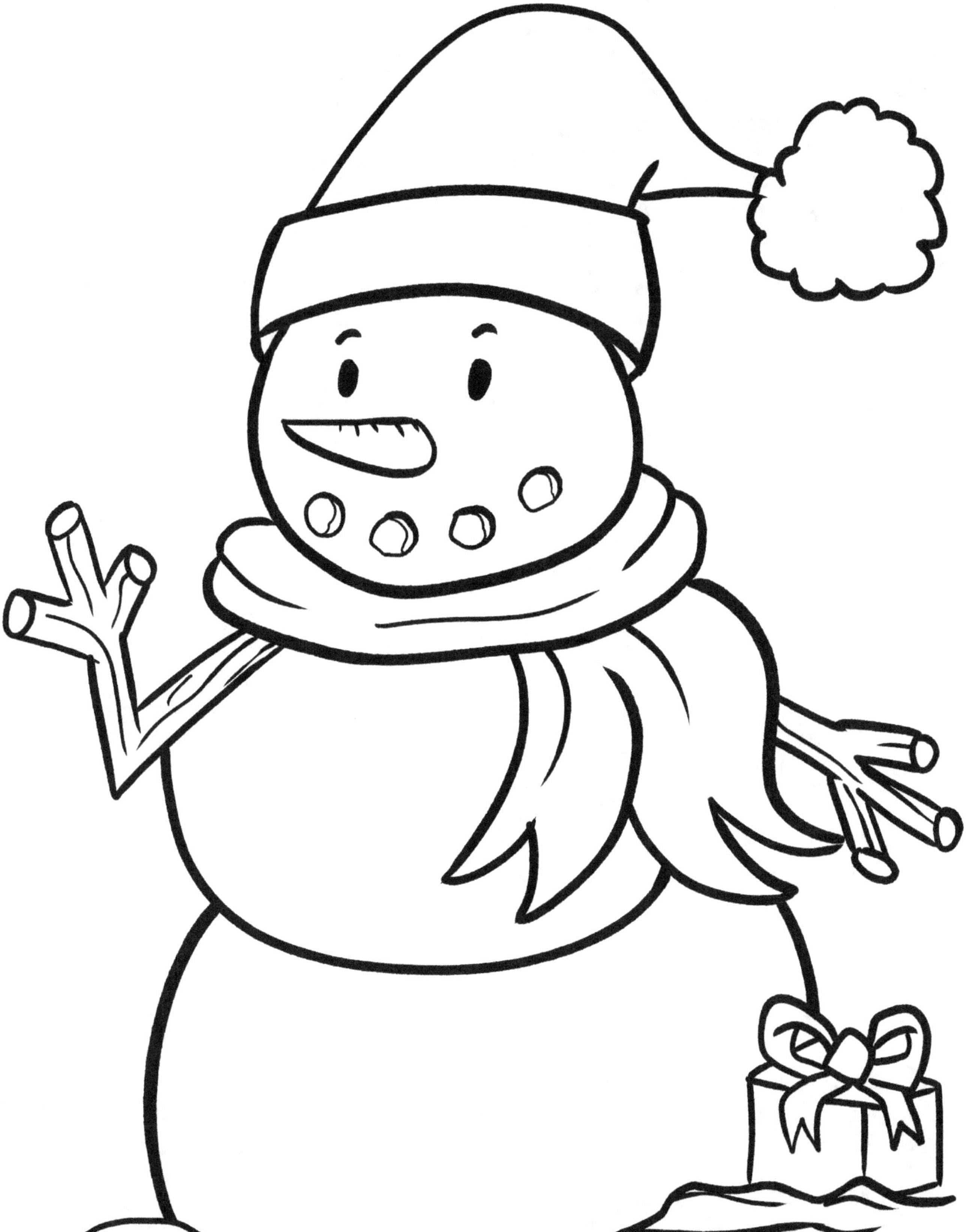

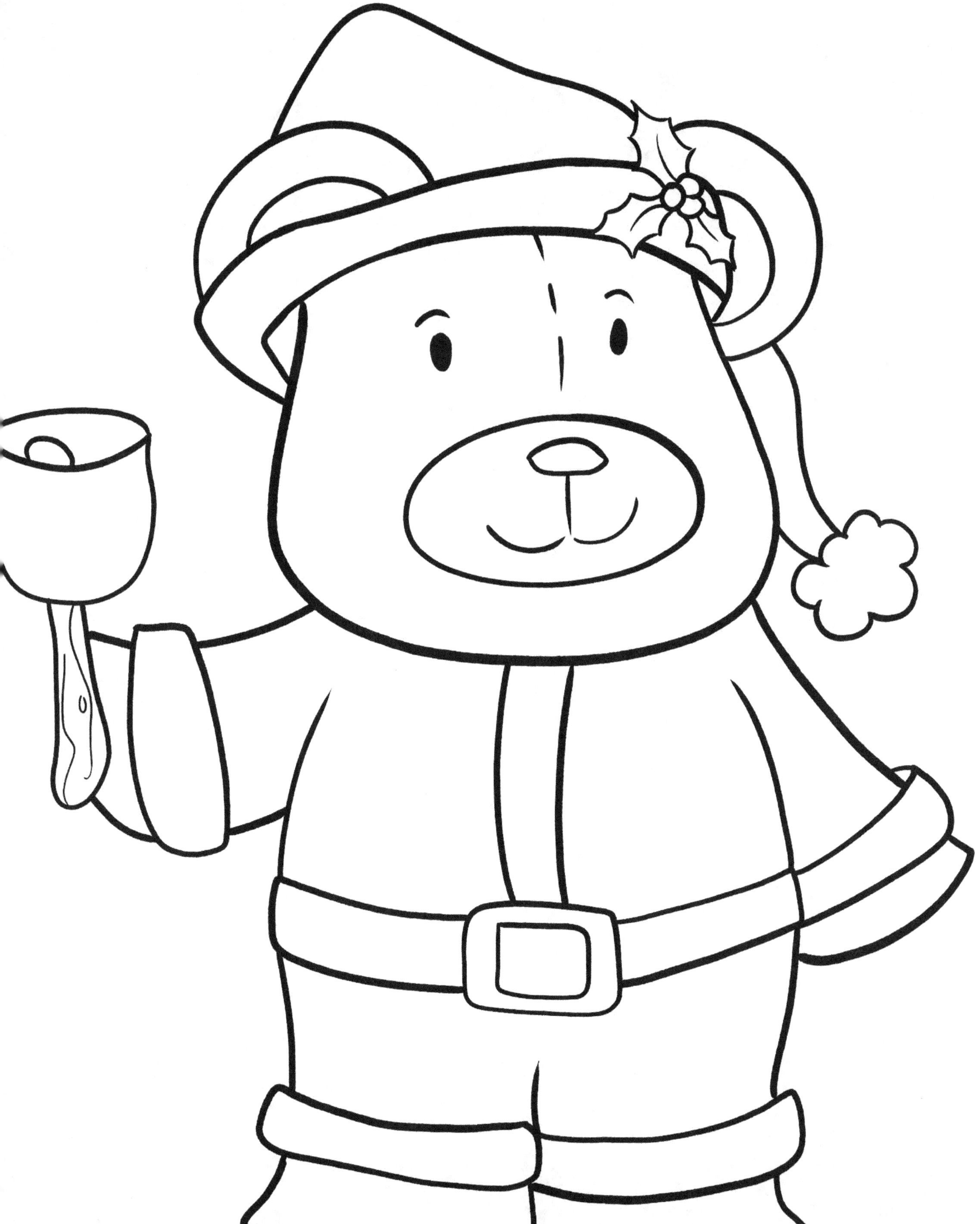

Solution

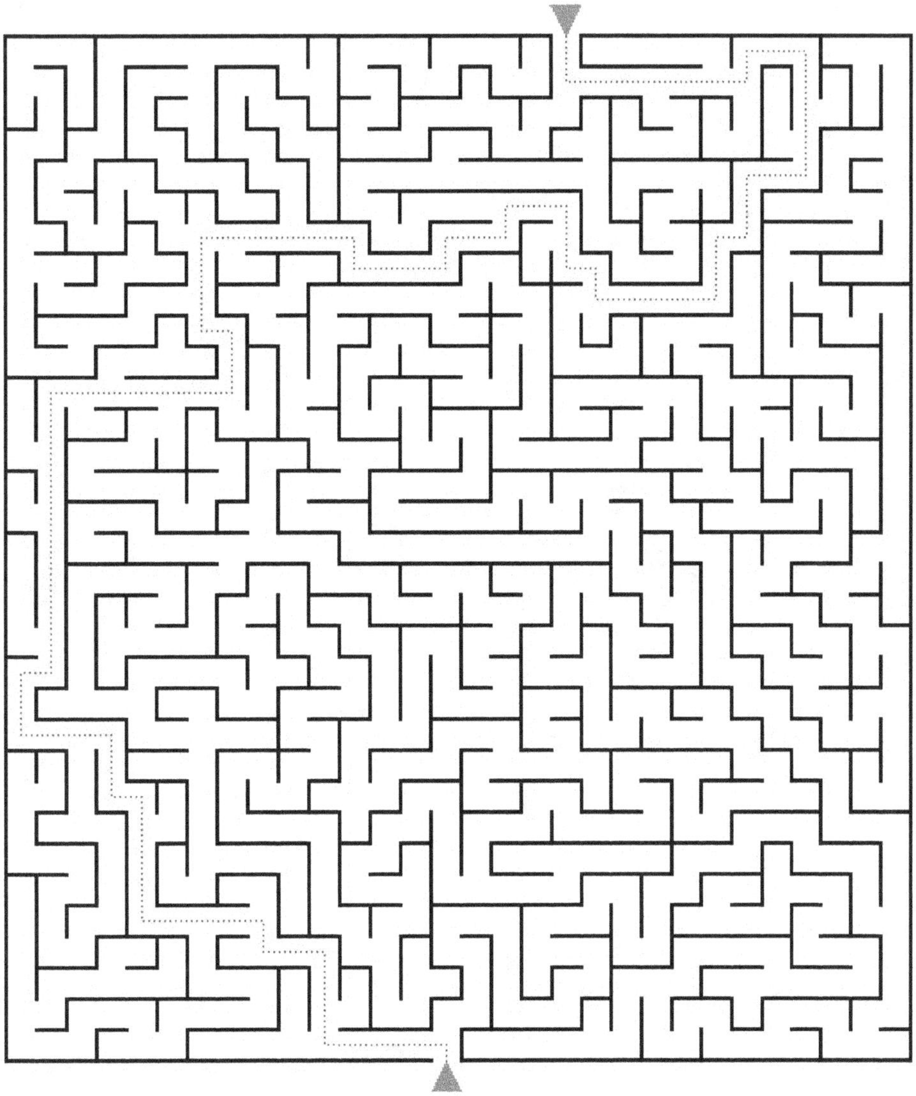

www.ingramcontent.com/pod-product-compliance
Lightning Source LLC
Chambersburg PA
CBHW080852220526
45467CB00008B/2478
* 9 7 8 1 7 0 5 5 9 1 1 3 0 *